FROM BAUHAUS TO BOWTIES

HGA CELEBRATES 35 YEARS

Bette Jones Hammel

HAMMEL GREEN AND ABRAHAMSON

Code for Abbreviations:

AIA	American Institute of Architects
ASHRAE	American Society of Heating, Refrigerating, and Air Conditioning Engineers
FAIA	Fellow American Institute of Architects
HSAE	Health Sciences Architects and Engineers
IT	Institute of Technology
MIT	Massachusetts Institute of Technology
MSAIA	Minnesota Society American Institute of Architects
NYU	New York University
P/A	Progressive Architecture magazine
PDT	Pillsbury Design Team
U of M	University of Minnesota

© 1989 by HGA, Hammel Green and Abrahamson, Inc.,

1201 Harmon Place, Minneapolis, Minnesota 55403

Library of Congress Catalog Card Number: 89-85989

ISBN-0-9622610-0-9

Manufactured in the United States of America.

CONTENTS

Foreward iv
Preface v

Chapter 1
Three Modernists Team Up 1

Chapter 2
Building a Reputation 11

Chapter 3
Early Challenges 19

Chapter 4
Turning Points 27

Chapter 5
Growing Pains 39

Chapter 6
Struggling Through The Recession 53

Chapter 7
On the Verge 65

Chapter 8
The 1980s Expansion 85

Chapter 9
New Landmarks for the Midwest 107

Chapter 10
Looking Toward the 21st Century 127

Acknowledgements 134

FOREWARD

Dick Hammel's untimely death shocked us into the realization that a portion of HGA's history had been lost. It was not our nature to celebrate anniversary years, but now thirty-five years in business took on a new significance. We were also challenged by a persistent Bette Hammel, Dick's wife and a professional writer, who said, "Gad, get it down so it won't be lost." It was only natural then that she became our author.

Countless hours extending over two years, interviewing and researching with staff and clients, past and present, has brought her personal style of writing about people to our book. In this case, it's those people who have made our architecture and engineering, our buildings, our personalities and humor, and our continuing practice.

To Bette, we owe a debt of gratitude that can only be expressed in a personal way — a big hug for what she's done for everyone who has been a part of our thirty-five years.

Assistance from our marketing staff — Janet Whitmore, Kim Dahlson, and Laura Collins — has been essential to progress and their work is more appreciated because these efforts were heaped on top of ongoing marketing projects.

The team of Hammel and Green, Bette Hammel and editor Ellen Green (no relation), has brought our story to print — an oddity worth mentioning.

— *Curt Green*

PREFACE

Architecture should uplift the human spirit, say the architectural historians. After writing this history (through laughter and tears), I now know how much emotion is packed into architecture. Dick said it succinctly in 1984, "We are designing for the celebration of human life."

This is the story of HGA's thirty-five high-spirited years. It is a story of people, remarkable people with divergent talents and personalities and, most of all great good humor who have directly contributed to this firm's steady growth.

Special thanks to: Curt Green, chairman of the history committee, for his generous input, moral support, and sensitive fine-tuning of this manuscript; to Bruce Abrahamson for his wit and style in relating HGA's architecture philosophy; to Jim Goulet and Harry Wilcox, who persisted in educating me about HGA engineers until I was convinced they could do almost anything; to Ted Butler, Julie Snow, and George Riches for editorial assistance; to Janet Whitmore for her creative help and production coordination; to Kim Dahlson for photography management; to Laura Collins and Wynne Mattila for script processing; to graphic designer Jim Johnson for enhancing the HGA spirit; and to editor Ellen Green for clamping down on my hyperbole.

— *Bette Jones Hammel*

FOR DICK

...Because architecture covers the whole field of human life, truly functionalist architecture must be functional primarily from the human point of view. If we look more closely at the progress of human life, we find that technology is only an aid and not a final and independent phenomenon in itself. Technical functionalism cannot achieve ultimate architecture.

— *Alvar Aalto*

CHAPTER ~ I

Curtis green Richard hammel Rolf n. irgens Bruce abrahamson David e. nordale George f. klein jr. Donald f. andrews Milwaukee public library Gilbert s. silverman Eugene l. freerks M. lee dahlen Marthea a. kimker Loren j. duerr Arthur o. haugsby Wayne r. winsor Walter gropius Harold f. schroeder Robert h. sperl Shirley c. hamilton Wes sorensen Winslow e. wedin Duane w. grande Mary tighe Chelsea heights elementary school Gary r. cook Mary l. gieske John bulov Jeanne m. thiry Arthur schaible Richard b. empey John p. salvatore Ludwig mies van der rohe John f. chisholm Donna m. gitzen Gerald w. froehlich Richard babcock Viona rice Merle r. lange Hugh g.s. peacock Howard lake school Robert c. havener Donna j. henaman Jack lindeman Leonard viehauser Pearl nangle William r. engelhardt Dwight o. churchill Eliel saarinen Robert l. beerstecher Ronald w. haase Charles d. malmer William b. stewart James moffat Brian r. morgan Gary n. afseth Earl anderson Albert g. voza Sigri a. sitz Curtis g. clarke Charles g. webb Doris e. werries Donna m. watson Charles b. thomsen Marcel breuer Charles l. miller Robert w. gish Glenn w. hawkinson Donald i. magnus David c. martin Patricia a. radford Culver d. whitcomb College of saint benedict Carl h. quist John budisalovich Arthur e. mcclure Gary a. cook Richard g. kern Fred loewen Robert a. keck Alvar aalto Douglas a. baird Theodore butler Jerry olson James sorenson Dan r. fox Dianna l. griffis James b. mcburney Saint paul schools Walter l. ware Robert l. kaster Donald k. melander James e. taplin Stephen s. reynolds Albert s. holmes Keith d. webster Skidmore owings & merrill Robert slaight Raymond a. diekman

Hammel and Green's first office in Curt Green's home.

CHAPTER 1

THREE MODERNISTS TEAM UP

Walter Gropius

Alvar Aalto and the Tuberculosis Sanatorium, Paimio, Finland

Along with other great changes that swept the United States after World War II, American architecture was breaking out of its long traditional mode. Modernism, or the International Style, which had developed in Europe in the 1920s and 1930s, was already making waves. With emphasis on simplicity and materials of steel, glass, aluminum, and concrete, Modernism swept away ornamentation, bringing structure and technology to the fore. Walter Gropius, Ludwig Mies van der Rohe, Eliel Saarinen, and Marcel Breuer were teaching the "new architecture" in leading architecture schools and influencing a new generation.

Among the students at Harvard University's highly influential Graduate School of Design, led by Gropius in the postwar years, were two young midwesterners, Richard Hammel and Bruce Abrahamson. Across Cambridge, Minneapolitan Curt Green studied at the Massachusetts Institute of Technology (MIT) under the direction of Finnish architect Alvar Aalto. The three students sensed they were in the forefront of an important movement and that there were exciting opportunities ahead.

America's built environment had many needs in the late 1940s and early 1950s for housing, schools, colleges, churches, hospitals, and offices. Leading Modernists met the demand with major works in large cities, buildings that proved to be of lasting influence on young architecture graduates. In Chicago, for example, Mies van der Rohe's twin apartment towers, "the glass houses" on Lake Shore Drive, were completed in 1951. On New York's Park Avenue, Lever House by Gordon Bunshaft of Skidmore Owings & Merrill also opened that year, followed by the Seagram Building by Mies and Philip Johnson in 1955. Both towers were considered milestones in Modernism.

In the Twin Cities of the early 1950s, there were three leading architectural firms — Ellerbe Architects, Inc.; Thorshov & Cerny; and Magney, Tusler & Setter (now Setter, Leach & Lindstrom, Inc.) — as well as three school specialists — Haarstick & Lundgren, Hubert Swanson & Associates, and Thorshov & Cerny. One of the young designers at Haarstick & Lundgren was tall, blue-eyed Curt Green, who quickly developed a reputation for design ability and hard work.

A classic example of Gropius' design

"Teamwork is simply a matter of love."
Gropius

CHAPTER 1

Curt Green

The only son of second-generation Minneapolis Swedes of modest means, Curtis H. Green grew up with an appreciation for hard work and high standards, a desire for higher education, and the drive to get ahead. He learned about color, crafts, and furniture from his father, Richard, who operated a custom furniture manufacturing shop. But he also came from his mother's mold and she loved to paint. As a youngster, he showed a love for color and design. In high school, he started to work in the *Minneapolis Star's* advertising department to save money for college, thinking he might pursue a career in advertising. On entering the University of Minnesota (U of M), however, he was counseled to pursue engineering. Green was determined that art should be a part of his life's work, so he arranged a meeting with Roy Jones, Head of the School of Architecture. The course descriptions convinced him that he should go into architecture.

Green first met Richard Hammel during his undergraduate years. Hammel was then in the U.S. Navy V-12 program in architecture and was already exhibiting leadership qualities on the All-U Council. "I still remember the illustrations he did, unusually logical and straightforward, but often humorous and flamboyant," said Green. Not until a few years later, when both men were on staff at the School of Architecture, did he and Hammel become friends.

Green graduated from the university within three years, in 1946. He landed his first architectural job with Magney, Tusler & Setter in Minneapolis and married his high school sweetheart, Marje Lee, in 1947. After receiving a fellowship for graduate study, he entered MIT, earning a master's degree in architecture in 1948. There Alvar Aalto became his mentor and idol. Although Aalto was a Modernist, he was also a humanist, exercising much more

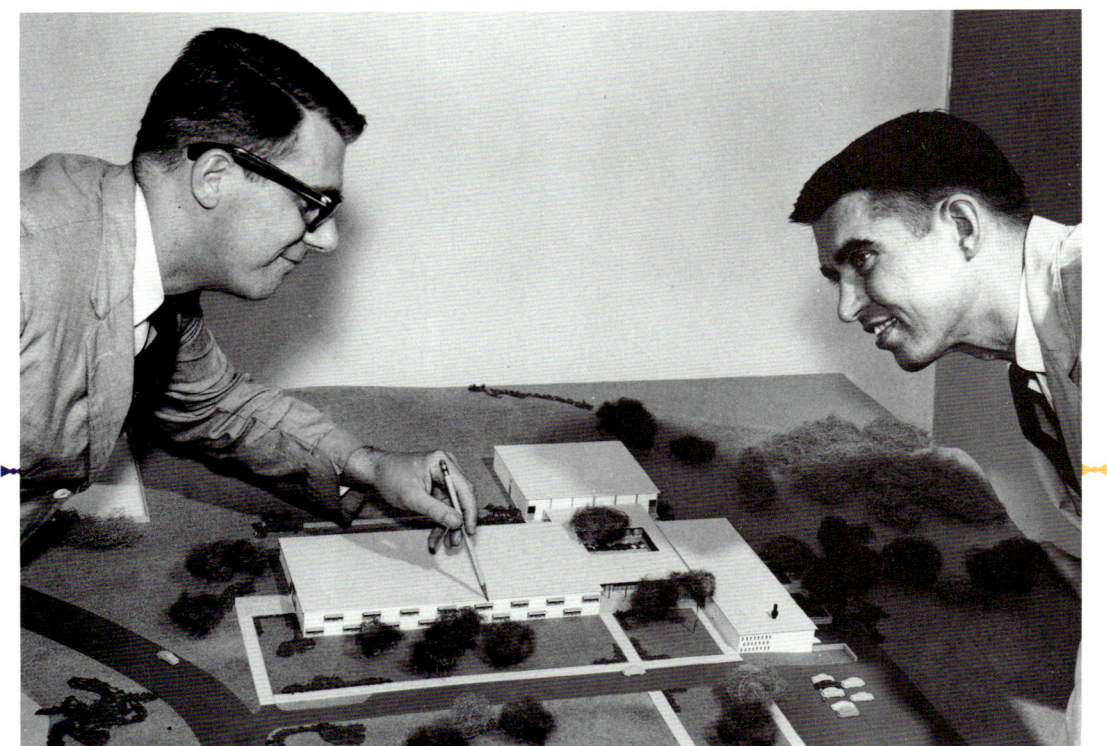

Hammel and Green discuss a new school design.

CHAPTER 1

freedom in his designs than the Bauhaus masters. "He always had a wiggle line in his designs for compositional relief and interest," Green recalled. Another professor who influenced the young architect was Ralph Rapson who critiqued the masters' class for a term. There was an excitement, a provocative newness, in his geometry and drawings that inspired Green.

Fresh out of MIT, Green accepted a post in Milwaukee where he designed an addition to the Milwaukee Public Library. Then seeking better opportunities supporting modern architecture, he moved back to Minnesota to join Thorshov & Cerny for a year and a half, then Haarstick & Lundgren for an equal stint. At these firms he worked on designs for the new Minneapolis General Hospital in 1950, a college library, and several schools. In addition, he taught part-time in the design studio at the U of M School of Architecture, where he again encountered Hammel.

Richard Hammel

Richard F. Hammel came from a family of builders in Owatonna, Minnesota. His grandfather, Louis, helped build the famous National Farmers Bank designed by Louis Sullivan. Richard's father, Erwin, initially a carpenter, went on to establish a concrete materials business and to become mayor of the town. As one of four sons, Richard (born in 1923) exhibited his intellectual capacities early, excelling in science and math while becoming president and valedictorian of his high school class. Recognizing that he also had artistic abilities, one teacher encouraged him to consider architecture as a career. His mother, Helen, of strong Czechoslovakian stock, backed him up.

After completing an architecture degree at the U of M in three years, Hammel graduated with distinction in 1944, then served in the U.S. Navy as a Lieutenant Junior Grade until 1946. After World War II he returned to his architectural studies at the Harvard Graduate School of Design, graduating in 1947 from Walter Gropius' master class. The Gropius influence permeated Hammel's general philosophy of architecture and his view of collaboration and teamwork. In applying for his first job, Hammel answered an ad to work in Honolulu with Richard Windisch, a German architect of the Bauhaus school. There, with a Korean designer and a Japanese architect, Hammel completed the office staff working in the Windisch house. In this office, he is said to have acquired his ability to draw upside down for clients seated across the table.

With opportunities in Hawaii limited and the cost of living high, Hammel returned to his native state after three years to accept a part-time teaching post at the U of M School of Architecture in 1950 and then a job as assistant consulting architect to the university. While working with architect Win Close, he was assigned to program University High School, his first chance to apply his technical and organizational skills to designing for education. Afterwards, he was hired by Magney, Tusler & Setter to design the school.

One year later, Hammel landed a job as consulting architect for the St. Paul Public Schools, then facing a crisis. With no real improvement since 1929, the schools had seriously deteriorated just as enrollment was soaring in 1950-51. Soon St. Paul's civic leaders reorganized the entire school system. A $9 million bond issue was passed for rehabilitating and remodeling existing schools and constructing six new elementary schools. J. Neal Morton, attorney and executive of the Briggs and Morgan law firm, was chairman of the St. Paul Board of Education, and Forrest

---

"I was scared stiff. We had just moved into a brand new house and had our second baby."
Marje Green

"Architecture is a verb and you have to do it."
Charles Jenks

CHAPTER 1

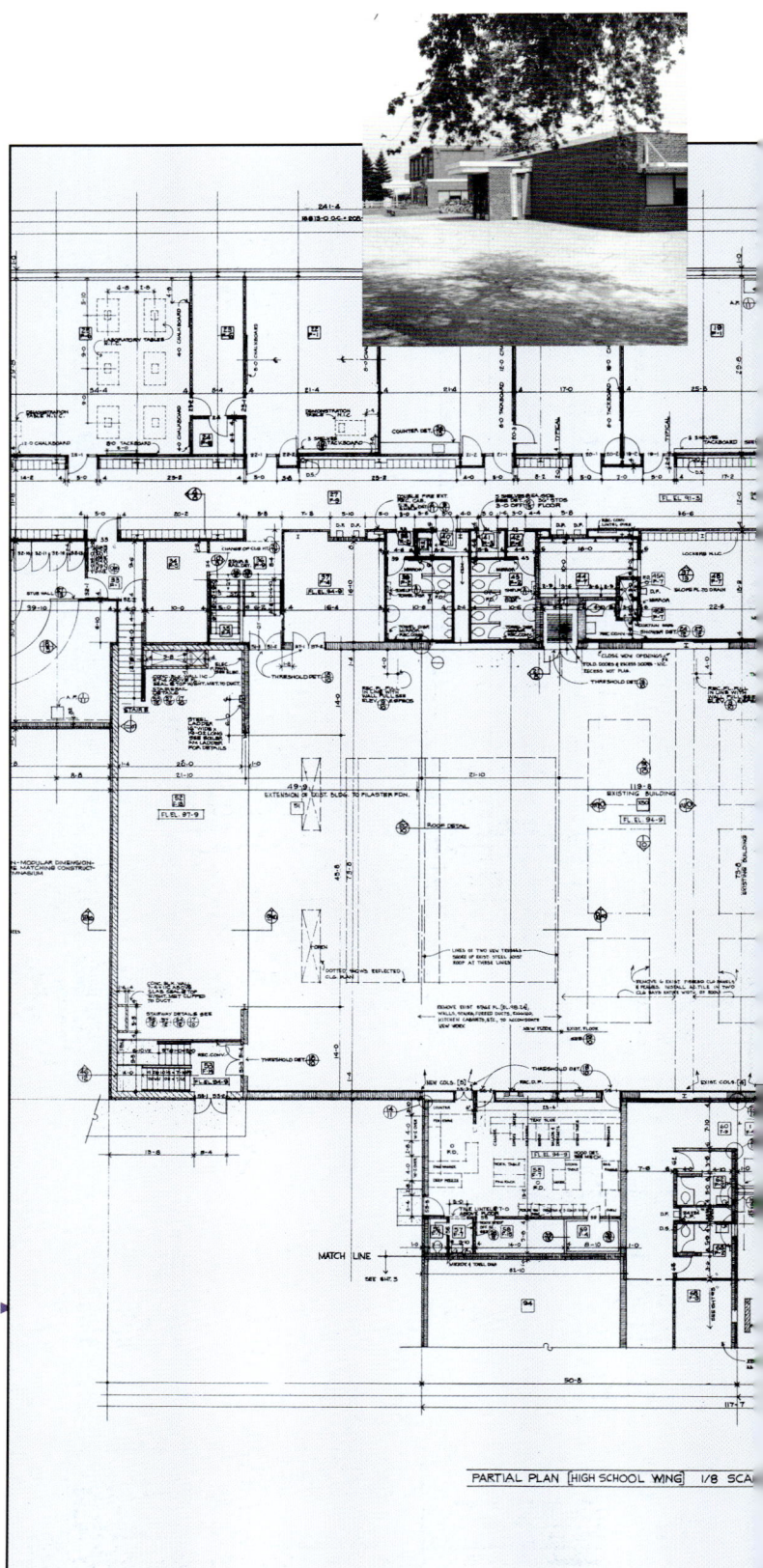

Conner was superintendent. Hammel was recommended, then hired, as staff architect to advise on the selection of local architects and school sites. "For a young man, Dick showed remarkable tact in the midst of all the politicking," reflected Morton.

The Chelsea Heights Elementary School addition brought Hammel and Green together, Green as architect for Haarstick & Lundgren, and Hammel as client, consulting architect for the St. Paul Board of Education. Working together, they discussed their ultimate goals, realizing they shared many ideas about practicing architecture.

In personality the two men were a contrast: the tall, thin black-haired Hammel with his wide, horn-rimmed spectacles gave the appearance of a scholar, the epitome of a Harvard man until he flashed his ready sense of humor. Green, warm and direct, always the sensitive artist-designer, by nature less outgoing than Hammel, but also fun-loving, impressed his friend with his determination and high ideals for improving the built environment.

The two young men, witnessing an incredible baby boom, knew the time was right for a new architectural firm. "Over lunch at the St. Paul Hotel in 1952, Dick and I agreed we knew almost everything about architecture and should set our own destiny," said Green. After another meeting, they decided to take on a job for a developer, Sauer Construction Company, preparing promotional designs for a shopping center. Working together more and more, they became increasingly serious about establishing their own practice.

In the spring of 1953, Zondal Miller, M.D. commissioned them to design his house on Upper St. Dennis Road in St. Paul. With just one commission, they could not afford to leave their

CHAPTER 1

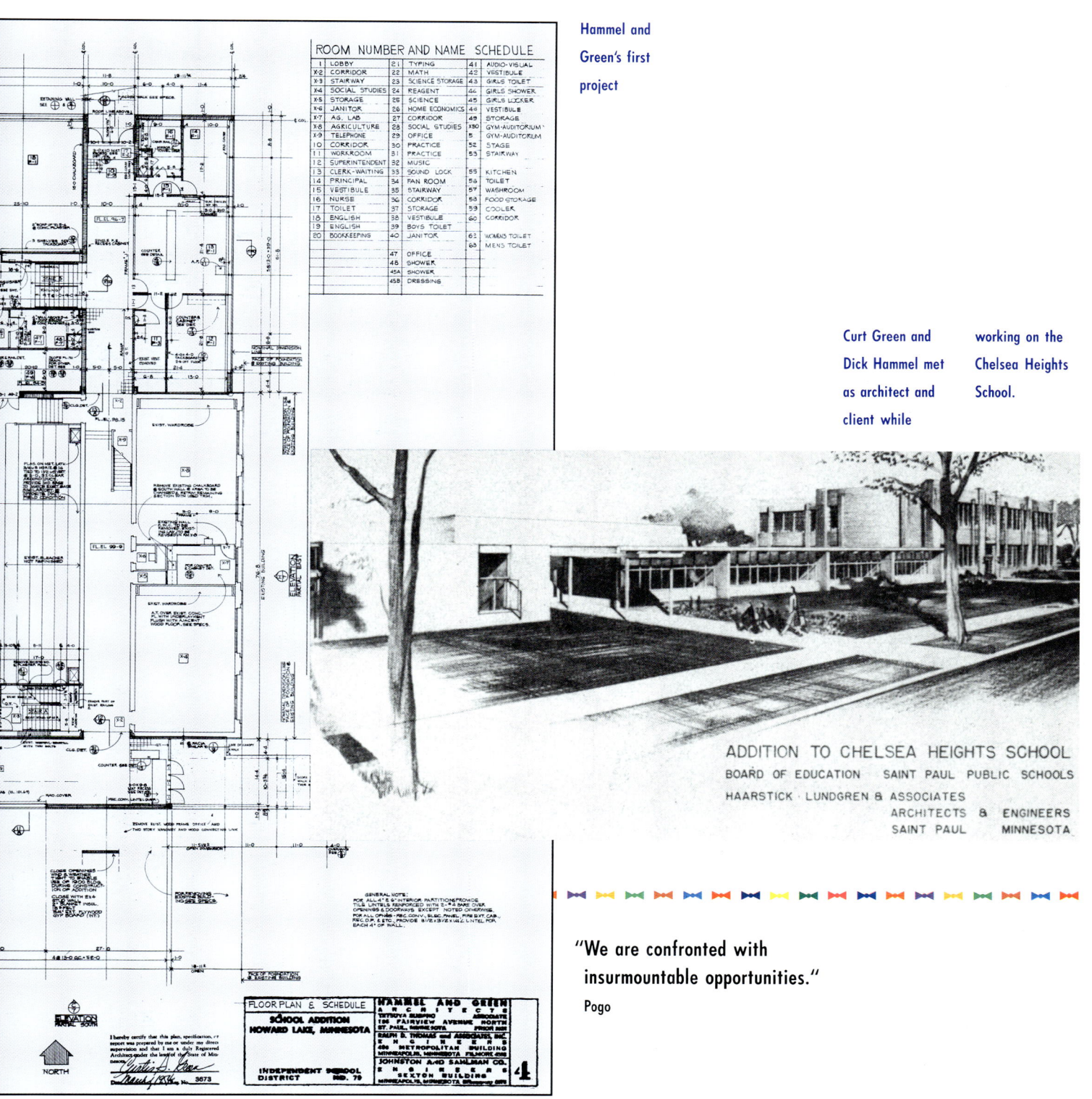

Hammel and Green's first project

Curt Green and Dick Hammel met as architect and client while working on the Chelsea Heights School.

"We are confronted with insurmountable opportunities."
Pogo

CHAPTER 1

respective places of employment, but began to make contacts for other prospective clients. Receiving encouragement, they decided to announce the formation of Hammel and Green in March 1953. Location? — the lower floor of Curt Green's house at 608 Turnpike Road in Golden Valley. Green resigned from his post, continuing to teach at the university through June; Hammel continued with the St. Paul Board of Education until then, too.

The decision was not made lightly. "I was scared stiff," said Marje Green. "We had just moved into a brand new house and had our second baby." Hammel and Green first set up their drawing boards in the playroom where they shared space with diapers hanging on a line. They promised to buy Marje a dryer with their first check.

The two entrepreneurs sought a school commission first. In March 1953, they began to pursue the Howard Lake School project, a $450,000 addition of elementary and secondary classrooms and a gym. The school superintendent, Earl Anderson, had attended Hammel's university class on school plant planning and was intrigued by his ideas. "Typically, the standard classrooms of the early 1950s were long, 24 x 36-foot spaces parallel to the corridor and always oriented to daylight," explained Green. "We proposed something new in school design — turning the classroom perpendicular to the corridor and using controlled fluorescent lighting all day," he said. (Hammel had developed this energy-saving idea with Lawrence E. "Duke" Johnson from Northern States Power Company while working on the University High project.)

Hammel and Green made sure the Howard Lake School Board toured the Chelsea Heights School, which illustrated their abilities as school architects, before the official interview in May 1953. After the presentation they waited anxiously for the Board's decision. When the members emerged, Hammel and Green had landed the job — its first. "Did we feel good!" recalled Green. The total fee was about $25,000 and with contract in hand, "We went right down to First National Bank of St. Paul, borrowed $3,000, and set out with a handshake to conquer the practice of architecture," he said. The Hammel and Green partnership was launched, and Marje Green got her new dryer!

The Howard Lake commission meant hiring consulting engineers for the first time, a major step in developing a policy emphasizing teamwork among architects, engineers, and clients. Milan Johnston of Johnston & Sahlman was retained as consulting structural engineer and R. D. Thomas & Associates for mechanical and electrical engineering.

The next commission, a hospital in Cumberland, Wisconsin costing $7,500 per bed, was constructed with a striking view of the rural landscape. Unfortunately, a patient wrote the architects that she could not see the beautiful "city" scene from her bed. That was the last time Hammel and Green heard from that healthcare client.

Meanwhile, the young firm learned that the College of St. Benedict, a small liberal arts college for women in St. Joseph, Minnesota, was going to build a 200-student dormitory, the school's first construction (excluding the power plant) since the chapel in 1912. Five Benedictine nuns made up the building committee, headed by Sister Magna Werth. Green, Hammel, and J. C. McMillan, an engineer from R. D. Thomas, went to the presentation armed with programming charts for the new dorm plus three site plan sketches showing how the campus could be expanded later. They had already struck a good response in talking to

> "In 1952, Dick and I agreed we knew almost everything about architecture and should set our own destiny."
> Curt Green

CHAPTER 1

students and sisters about the social structure and requirements for the dormitory. This concept of programming was new to the sisters. Through Hammel's work with the St. Paul schools, he had developed a system for programming schools: setting goals and space requirements, listing all the rooms, and the needs of teachers, students, and the physical plant. In the presentation to St. Benedict's, Hammel and Green proved they had done their homework. In December 1953 they were awarded the design for Mary Hall. It was their first million-dollar-plus commission! The two confident young architects could now afford to move out of Green's basement. They knew they had to relocate to be considered for a St. Paul school project, so, fired with ambition and great plans, Hammel and Green rented a former barbershop at 186 North Fairview in St. Paul. They moved in the fall of 1953.

With major commissions in hand, Hammel and Green hired its first designer, Ted Sugano, a graduate of the U of M and Harvard. As more opportunities appeared, the architects decided they needed another top-flight designer. Green's first thought was to call Bruce Abrahamson, whose work he had admired at Thorshov & Cerny, and lure him away from the Chicago office of Skidmore Owings & Merrill.

Bruce Abrahamson, The Third Partner

Growing up in the depression years of the 1930s in north Minneapolis, Bruce A. Abrahamson learned to draw and paint under the guidance of his father, Clifford, a man of Norwegian descent with artistic talents used both at work and at home. Clifford had worked for the Minneapolis Park Board as a crafts supervisor and for General Mills Engineering Department during the war years. "He fueled the fire in me that ignited my devotion

Dick Hammel, warm yet direct, tough yet compassionate, was a natural leader who led the office for years with wit and charisma. Ever the intellectual, Hammel was known for his keen ability to grasp a problem quickly, arrive at a solution, and make a decision.

Curt Green, concerned and earnest, was a sensitive artist who commanded respect, taking personal delight in every successful project. Always the Scandinavian gentleman, he provided design strength through the years. Conceptualizing projects quickly was his forte.

Bruce Abrahamson, lively and fun, a jaunty professorial type, often wore an engaging grin as he led his design teams through heated debates. Adept at articulating his thoughts on architecture, he became known as the trio's great arbitrator.

"At 25, I was ready to sell my soul, my wife and all I had for a Barcelona chair. I believed then that less just had to be more."
Bruce Abrahamson

CHAPTER 1

and commitment to a life in visual design," Bruce said.

For two years before college, he served in the Naval Air Force, where the rigorous discipline and hard training left a lifelong impression. After the war Abrahamson enrolled at the U of M with the idea of becoming an industrial designer. On discovering the School of Architecture, he was thoroughly swept up in the field, graduating with distinction in 1949. During Abrahamson's college years, Professor Robert G. Cerny hired him for part-time work in his firm, further influencing Abrahamson's career.

In 1950 Abrahamson was awarded a scholarship to the Harvard Graduate School of Design, where he became a student of "the Silver Prince". Abrahamson reflected, "My teacher, Walter Gropius, was revered in my life then, and his teachings remain today as a guide in my philosophy and approach to architecture". After earning his master's degree, Abrahamson was awarded the prestigious Rotch Traveling Scholarship and spent an exciting year in Europe. He returned to the United States to accept a job offer from Skidmore Owings & Merrill of Chicago.

At that time, Mies van der Rohe was working in Chicago, and Abrahamson wanted to learn from the master. "While working with the academic elite, I was invited to Mies' house and, with other aspiring architects, sat at his feet with my eyes watering from his cigar smoke, knowing I was in Mecca," recalled Bruce. "At 25, I was ready to sell my soul and all I had for a Barcelona chair. I believed simplicity was holiness and less just had to be more."

Just about this time, Curt Green invited Abrahamson to join the new firm in St. Paul. "Hammel and Green was a dynamic young office with design as its motivation. They were just getting started and what appealed to me was the opportunity to help shape it and grow with it," said Abrahamson. He joined the firm early in 1954. With his big-firm sophistication and design talents, he soon became a major force in the Hammel and Green office.

Now there were three — Dick Hammel, Curt Green, and Bruce Abrahamson — each with a strong character, a clear vision, and deep convictions about architecture. They shared a common philosophy, firmly believing in the team concept of architecture espoused by Gropius. They were convinced that good architecture is the result of multi-disciplined talents focusing together under a principal architect's leadership.

Despite common goals, the three leaders differed from one another in personality and style. Nevertheless, they complemented one another and developed a deep respect as they worked together over the years. Known as "the troika", they did not believe in the "hero" type of architecture, and resolved never to build up any one name over the other. This team spirit became the basis for the firm's success. With Abrahamson aboard, Hammel and Green had a first-class team.

Gropius and Abrahamson

"Architectural teams are like a string of pearls — composed of readily distinguishable individuals, tied together in unity of purpose."
Bill Caudill

CHAPTER ~ II

Ronald H. Hancock John J. Sperberg John C. Towner Douglas W. Foster Edward J. Vogt Highland Park Junior High Marvin W. Johnson Reynold M. Roberts David J. Bennett Duane H. Temple Gary Hall George E. McGuire Fredric E. Melby Paul Rudolph Brian R. Wessel Mary L. Pehaski John E. Rudquist Dale E. Dzubay Calvin K. Anderson Gary J. Anderson Rodney Erickson Owatonna school board Jeffery C. Rice Richard J. Carlson Peter R. Lee Roger C. Freeberg John M. Mackay John C. Gaunt John B. Prentis Eero Saarinen Stanley E. Pinska Ingrid Weiland Ali A. Vahhaji Thomas J. Jennings Louanne Thomas Carolyn Stolson Kenneth Schultz Ellendale schools Thomas M. Ulrich James Moffat Linda L. Anderson Takiaki Toyoma Geoffrey W. Carlson Robert Schwartz Carolyn R. McKelvey Le Corbusier Theodore A. Podolske James Wengler Brenton D. Tibbetts Donald E. Flynn Harry Wilcox Barbara J. Mikel Pillsbury company Daniel C. Larson Stephen J. Hammel Rosalin Gardner Vern E. Svedberg Eldon Burow Larry J. Hurlbut Frank Lloyd Wright Michael J. Fitzgibbon Duane Blanchard William Haaversen Kathleen A. Frazee Allen S. Weiss Robert S. Takaichi James H. Ehlke Albert Lea schools Jack D. Smuckler Donald D. Black Vincent F. Bastian Alfred W. French III Calvin M. Niemeyer Joseph J. Vano William R. Engelhardt Stillwater schools Gary L. Lewis Sharon R. Bohnhoff Jerrald Olson Richard F. Zenisek Richard B. Morrill Kenneth S. Halpern Walter Johnson Tom Campbell Noel M. Knudson Gregory P. Molitor Mario Averbuj William Pothen John P. Ensrude David N. Constable George Eklund Willmar state hospital Linden B. Carr Allen A. Ambrose Duane A. Kell Jack A. Carr William Anderson Robert L. Morgan Robert Parupsky Arthur Naftalin George W. Orth

CHAPTER II

BUILDING A REPUTATION

Mary Hall
College of St. Benedict

The baby boom of the early 1950s created an urgent need for new schools and a demand for development throughout the United States. Good buildings were badly needed and modern architecture was now being accepted, though some clients still resisted. Many bad imitations of good modern architecture were constructed much to the dismay of qualified designers. Hammel and Green was determined to do only quality work with modern materials and the latest innovations in modern technology — always with the client's needs in mind.

After only a year, Hammel and Green had acquired a reputation as an architectural firm with fresh ideas. "Regionally, we represented a new direction in the architecture world," said Bruce Abrahamson. "We wanted to do good work, and if we were not the right size to handle what came along, we would hire more people to help. We had a commitment to design." The partners shared a common goal — that together they could do something strong. All three principals agreed that the creative interchange of a professional team, individuals highly skilled in their own disciplines, could produce the best architecture. That philosophy set the firm apart.

With the Howard Lake School addition (underway in 1954) illustrating many of its new ideas in school design, the young firm pressed for more school work. The Owatonna School Board soon awarded Hammel and Green three elementary additions, and another project for the Ellendale schools followed. With their hot new designer Abrahamson, the partners pooled ideas and came up with innovations such as interior courts, flexible floor plans, lots of color, attractive classrooms, fun spaces for students, and controlled daylight for consistent light levels. Many of these ideas helped save construction dollars.

Word of Hammel and Green's new approach had by now spread around the community. Shortly after moving into the Fairview storefront, they received a call from the St. Paul Town and Country Club's Building Committee about a new clubhouse. An interview date was set and the staff scrambled to finish remodeling its new office. The day before the anticipated date, they were installing paneling in the store window as a display space for drawings when the Town and Country

CHAPTER II

Highland Park Junior High School

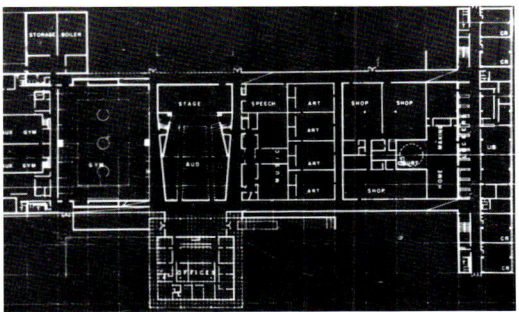

The baby boom of the 1950s brought a wealth of new projects for the young architectural firm.

Club Building Committee, including several prominent St. Paul businessmen, unexpectedly appeared. The young architects were caught completely unprepared. Hammel and Green did not get the commission though the incident caused many a laugh for years.

Early in 1954 came the firm's first chance for a corporate job. The Pillsbury Company wanted to remodel and expand its research and development laboratories in southeast Minneapolis. Since Abrahamson had already taken part in elaborate programming for Motorola Corporation and other corporate giants while working for Skidmore Owings & Merrill, it was a perfect marketing opportunity. He got the commission and did all the design work, completing the remodeling the following year. Meanwhile, Curt Green carried on with final designs for Mary Hall, the dormitory at the College of St. Benedict.

Highland Park Junior High School

About this same time, Hammel was pursuing a project funded by a 1953-54 bond issue for the St. Paul Board of Education. Hammel's former boss, Forrest Conner, was still School Superintendent and Neil Morton still Chairman of the School Board. They remembered Hammel's early administration of school construction, and soon Hammel and Green won the commission to design Highland Park Senior High School for 900 students.

This metropolitan school project, Hammel and Green's first, was a turning point. Hammel was principal architect and Abrahamson, project designer. "We really put many of our innovative ideas into Highland," said Green. "We stacked the classrooms in one three-story building, all narrow to the corridor and to the outside. By eliminating the traditional scheme of long corridors and wings, we saved 60 square feet per classroom. That cut

"No one does anything around here alone."
HGA Anonymous

HAMMEL GREEN AND ABRAHAMSON

CHAPTER II

needless steps, increased efficiency, and reduced the amount of land needed. Cutting down corridor space and subsequent building size meant we could build quality schools for less. This concept enabled us to do a wide school building rather than a long narrow school that cost more." Other innovations included special department designs in which departments such as music, home economics, science, and shop were grouped together in an efficient square-shaped wing, with perimeter corridors on each side. The corridors became thermal barriers, controlling sunlight to the interior. Both students and teachers could enjoy the view outdoors while moving between classes.

Exterior freshness was achieved through color and modern materials — bright orange, glazed brick and blue metal panels in a glass curtain wall. "I believed that buildings should express to the world what they are all about and that you should be able to get a hint about what's happening inside," said Abrahamson. Working on these schools in the Fairview rehabbed barbershop, the Hammel and Green team — Hammel, Green, Abrahamson, and designers James Stageberg, Rolf Irgens, and David Nordale — sat in one room working on every aspect of the project. This informal work environment became a company tradition.

With a need for housing, churches, schools, and other institutional facilities, the 1950s were reasonably good years for architects. Some clients were reluctant to accept modern architecture, so "we had to sell the designs we did, and if you had to spend an extra dime to do so, it may have been a wasted dime," recalled Abrahamson. "Still, a lot of clients were receptive to logical solutions, like simplified floor plans and clean, colorful exteriors."

Highland Park Junior and Senior High Schools

CHAPTER II

Albert Lea Schools

Hammel and Green was winning recognition in the educational field just as a major opportunity arose in southern Minnesota. The Albert Lea school district had just passed a $4 million bond issue, and Hammel and Green quickly lined up an interview. After many trips to Albert Lea, the firm was awarded the commission in 1954. John "Jake" Halverson, Albert Lea superintendent of schools, later commented that Hammel and Green provided a refreshing contrast to other architects in listening to the needs of the school district and its administration. Rather than imposing their own ideas, the designers indicated a willingness to learn.

The Albert Lea project was huge for the young firm, so it immediately staffed up to meet the challenge. Early in 1955, the partners added another Minnesota graduate, George Klein Jr., a persuasive Canadian who fit right in with the genial atmosphere and high goals of the group. The affable James Stageberg, fresh out of the Harvard Graduate School of Design, had already joined the staff. Other architects hired that year included Donald Hustad, Eugene Freerks, and Gilbert Silverman. Draftsman M. Lee Dahlen, hired for his technical and field experience, would prove invaluable. Seeing a need and filling it, Dahlen took over the writing of construction specifications, establishing that job as a vital part of company services.

John J. Halverson Elementary School

The John J. Halverson Elementary School in Albert Lea, (originally known as Southeast Elementary) was a rectangular building of brick with small window bands and exposed steel and aluminum. A library in the center had glazed walls facing both corridors. James Stageberg was the designer. In 1956 the school

Lee Dahlen

Southwest Junior High School
Albert Lea

Green and Hammel talking over some new ideas

"I drove my '53 Olds and beat the bushes calling on school districts around the state."
Curt Green

HAMMEL GREEN AND ABRAHAMSON

CHAPTER II

won an award from *Progressive Architecture*.

The time had come to move out of the crowded Fairview office. In 1955, Hammel and Green moved to 1932 ½ University Avenue, occupying the floor above a saw repair shop. The staff now numbered about 12 architects and a secretary/bookkeeper, all working in one big space. "We did everything — pitching in on design, renderings, working drawings, construction supervision, shop drawings, administration — whatever was necessary to complete the work," recalled Green. "All of us were trying our very best to make waves in architecture."

Austin Schools

In 1955, the firm acquired another major school district commission, this time from Austin, Minnesota. Having won the confidence of superintendent Leif Harbo, business manager Len Coumbe, and the Austin Board of Education, Hammel and Green set to work on the new Ellis Junior High School, an elementary school, and three additions.

The innovative school, appearing to be just one story from the exterior, actually had a two-story interior. Working with an unwieldy site on poor soil, designer Hugh Peacock centered the first level around a two-level open courtyard. The exterior showed a Miesian influence with its exposed steel columns and a black and white curtain wall. Arched "cafetorium" entrances and interior windows gave the space distinction. Unfortunately, Ellis was later destroyed by fire.

Stillwater Schools

As the firm's reputation spread, Dick Hammel and Curt Green increasingly sought interviews with school districts. In 1956 the company was hired to remodel Stillwater Senior High, which had been partially demolished in a fire. Then came another major project — design a new senior high school and convert the old one to a junior high. Principal architect Hammel and designer Hugh Peacock worked closely with Superintendent Tom Campbell. Campbell had encountered Hammel at a National School Administrators convention in Atlantic City in 1952. Campbell wrote:

I was attending a panel discussion and there was a tall, skinny, black-haired guy with horned rims and ivy league tweeds continually asking questions. Not only that, he seemed to have all the answers. A few years went by, and in 1958 I was superintendent of Stillwater's district and was waiting for a visit from the "school" architect, as they called him. He soon ambled in. Here was the same owlish-looking guy in the ivy league tweeds! It was Hammel all right. That began a friendship of 28 years. Building for education in Minnesota profited greatly because of Dick Hammel's abiding dedication . . . He was uniquely the "school" architect.

Incorporation

With prospects bright and risks increasing, Hammel and Green decided to incorporate. The first Articles of Incorporation were signed on May 22, 1956, for Hammel and Green, Incorporated, by Richard F. Hammel, Curtis H. Green, and Frank Graham, an attorney with Briggs, Gilbert, Morton, Kyle & Macartney (later Briggs and Morgan).

Among employees joining the staff in 1956 were Wesley

"You saw a need and you did it."
Lee Dahlen

"Lee minded the store."
Bruce Abrahamson

CHAPTER II

Ludwig Mies Vander Rohe

Dick Hammel

Ellis Junior High

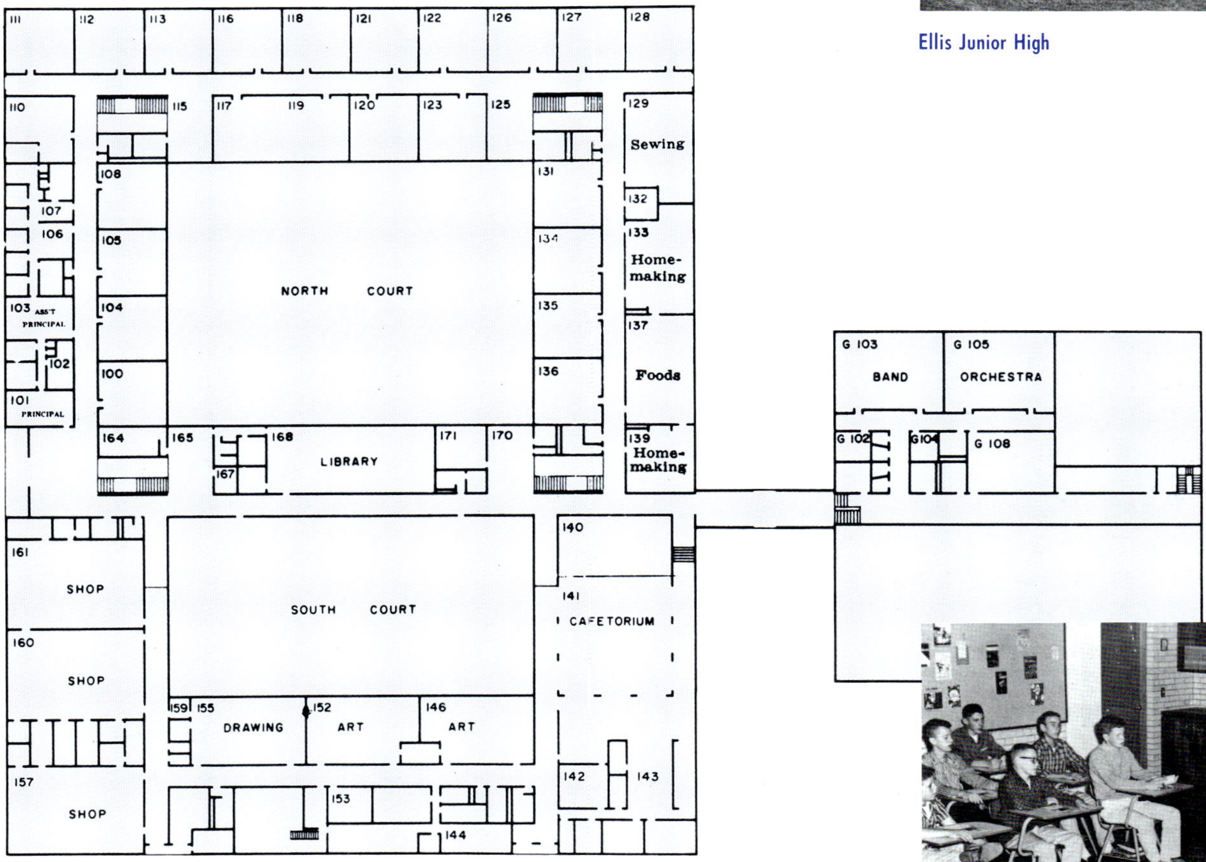

Students enjoy the new music room at Ellis Junior High

"Never trust a man who wears a bow tie.
HGA Anonymous

HAMMEL GREEN AND ABRAHAMSON

CHAPTER II

George Klein Jr.

The office staff always enjoyed in-house 'seminars'.

Sorensen, project architect on dozens of Hammel's school projects, Gary Cook, John Duerr, Duane Grande, Harold Schroeder, Robert Sperl, Winslow Wedin, and Wayne Winsor. By the end of 1956, the firm numbered 20 employees, but by April 1957, business was slow and the staff had to be reduced to 14.

"No matter what, it was a fun-loving office," recalled Mary Tighe, who began as a secretary in 1956 and 35 years later is specification's production manager. "We always had students working for us, so there were times you'd find goldfish in the water-cooler...Because we worked so closely, we always knew the exact status of each job. We knew Hammel and Green was a good design firm, and we worked very hard because we had such pride in our work. It was a real team effort."

While the informal work atmosphere remained, corporate structuring meant officers had to be elected and management meetings held on a regular basis. Hammel became President and Green, Chairman of the Board of Directors. Abrahamson became First Vice President, Ralph Irgens, Secretary, and George Klein and Hugh Peacock, Vice Presidents.

First Branch Office, Austin

At the August 1956 meeting, the board made a brave move — opening an office in Austin, Minnesota with George Klein as project manager for the Austin public schools. Klein and his family moved to Austin where he had his work cut out for him. "We had a thriving practice in Austin for three years," recalled Klein, "including small office buildings, houses, and the Red Cedar Inn." The route between St. Paul and Austin was heavily traveled because of Hammel and Green's commitment to the southwestern Minnesota community.

"Never had so much been done by so few."
Mary Tighe

CHAPTER - III

C. VAUGHN ANDERSON LANCE A. LAVINE LESTER J. VALL RUSSELL W. RINGSAK ANNA DEHLIN DAVID R. HILL STATE COLLEGE BOARD ROBERT L. RODRIGUEZ RONALD E. PETERSON PERRY BOLIN GAYLE F. VON WALD JOHN P. VAN DYKE PAUL D. FINSNESS LINDA M. SCHUMACHER UNIVERSITY OF MINNESOTA ERIC J. UTNE MICHAEL P. LOGAN NORMAN B. LIVGARD EMALEE J. HAYDEN LYNDA R. CROMER LAUREN P. CLUCKEY MERLE M. MYERS STAN HUBBARD JUDITH A. GAGE BRUCE V. TUNELL LAURENCE S. PERRA JOHN MULLOY LARRY D. SOBERG DONALD J. SUPPES PATRICIA A. DEAVEN CLAUDE H. BLACK JR. JONATHAN T. MILLER DENNIS W. BLAGER SUE L. NORRIS ELIZABETH M. NELSON DONALD E. VERMELAND DONALD E. WHEELER SAINT BEDE'S PRIORY GARY L. JACOBSON KEVIN E. MAYNARD JAMES GOULET MARY J. MANDELKOW JOHN S. WEEKS RICHARD F. KOEHN JED PHROMYOTHI ROSEMOUNT SCHOOL DISTRICT #196 CATHERINE M. CORNELL CYNTHIA A. POOLER THEODORE K. STEINER PAUL REYELTS WILLIAM C. WINDER DONALD W. SYLVESTER JAMES T. AITKEN THE DONALDSON COMPANY ROWLAND C. HAND, JR. GERALD L. GRANT KIETH G. JOHNSON THOMAS C. CLARKE JERRALD OLSON ROBERT W. WALSH, JR. CHELSEA HEIGHTS ELEMENTARY SCHOOL GARY R. COOK JOHN E. DOLEZILEK FRANK DONALDSON GLENN W. HAWKINSON LINDA ANDERSON VAN SCOTT NIENOW ROBERT D. MACKIE WAYNE J. SISEL LINDA A. MAKINEN PRAKASH KOTAK MINNEAPOLIS CLINIC OF PSYCHIATRY AND NEUROLOGY HOLLYCE L. GREEN RONALD C. ERICKSON JAMES A. CAMPBELL RAGNWALD BOLSTAD SUSAN C. HAND DONALD F. MEIER WILLIAM HOWARD SAINT PAUL SKYWAYS RICHARD G. DILLON RONALD W. BUELOW JEFFREY C. JOHNSON SALOMON M. RIVKIN SHASHI M. SURI KURT ROGNESS PATRICK M. SULLIVAN LUTHERAN CHURCH OF THE REFORMATION WILLIAM J. ROTHMAN GEORGE AHTOU JAMES R. KOONCE GALEN GRANT DAVID M. BENSTON DAVID A. HENDERSON

CHAPTER III

EARLY CHALLENGES

Knowing how vital it was to have creative engineers working directly with their architects, Hammel and Green decided it was time to establish an in-house engineering department. The new materials and technology of modern architecture called for engineering innovations as well as architectural ones. "We wanted to spread architectural creativity into engineering, so the spark of the building came through everywhere," said Green.

For the first three years, the firm hired consulting engineers — R. D. Thomas for mechanical and electrical engineering and Johnston-Sahlman for structural. Milan Johnston and John Sahlman had worked particularly closely with Hammel and Green on early educational projects. Milan Johnston first met Richard Hammel while Johnston was teaching at the U of M. "Hammel was by far the brightest member of my class," recalled Johnston. "I'll never forget what he said to me when he finished the course: 'I have to stay in the navy for a while, but someday I'm going to have my own office and you are going to be my structural engineer.'"

George Klein and Dick Hammel set off to advise another state college.

After incorporation, the first order of business was to discuss bringing in engineers. A search committee was organized then, but not until January 1959 did the company, despite financial pressures, hire its first staff mechanical engineer, Robert Gish. Later that fall, David Martin became the staff's first electrical engineer.

"In hiring engineers, we made a major decision — to become a full-service firm," said Abrahamson. The board also decided to re-identify the firm as Hammel and Green Architects & Engineers, Inc. Engineers became an official part of the total design process and integral members of the in-house design team in October 1959. The collaboration of engineers with architects helped set the firm apart, and as architecture became more exploratory, Hammel and Green set a course to use new technology in more creative ways.

"It was a sound business decision to expand the base of the business," said Harry Wilcox, longtime head of the engineering department. "Since engineering can be up to 50 percent of the value of what's done in terms of design, it could generate another source of income for the firm."

"God is in the details."
Mies van der Rohe

CHAPTER III

The State of Minnesota

To keep the firm moving ahead, the principals were always looking for new business. Green and Hammel described potential projects as "anything that bears a fee." Since Hammel had already established good contacts with school superintendents throughout the state and the firm was recognized in the educational field, the two architects decided it was time to call on the State of Minnesota and the Office of the State Architect in pursuit of a major commission. It came in the form of a building to house food service and laundry facilities for the Willmar State Hospital in 1955. Principal Green and designer Hugh Peacock designed a plan with four walls of windows. The state bought the plan even though it was a new concept for the state hospital system then.

State College Board

In the mid-1950s, Minnesota's five state colleges needed major updating and repair. On all five campuses, then bulging with increased enrollments, physical plants had deteriorated. Arthur Naftalin (later mayor of Minneapolis) was State Commissioner of Administration in late 1954. At the request of Governor C. Elmer Anderson, he put together a budget for the renovation of the colleges, receiving $27 million from the 1956 legislature. An interim Commission, chaired by Naftalin, was appointed to study state educational building needs. The Commission asked for, and got, $54 million in the 1957-59 biennium.

"As Commissioner of Administration, I was dealing with five different colleges, each competitive, each with a different director," recalled Naftalin. "So I came up with the brilliant idea of hiring Hammel as the consulting architect for the State College Board and giving him the job of supervising the architects chosen to work with each college." There was a tendency at that time to give work to old, well-established Minnesota architects, but Naftalin was looking for younger firms with fresh ideas. Of these, he knew that Hammel and Green had the most experience in education. "Dick had a personal style that was not brittle. He was straightforward and rational and carried it off with good humor," said Naftalin.

In 1957, Hammel became consulting architect for the State College Board in a milestone project that continued through three administrations until 1968 and generated steady income for the firm. Working closely with Hammel on the project was partner George Klein. Klein was also a pilot so for longer trips (Bemidji, Moorhead, Marshall, and Winona), he flew a single-engine Beechcraft Bonanza. "I remember one time when we two city-slickers from St. Paul had flown to Bemidji for an important meeting at the college, then hurriedly grabbed a cab for Sattgast Hall. Upon arriving, we both reached in our pockets...no cash! The bill was 60 cents. So Dick reached for the cabbie's pencil stub and with a grand flourish wrote out a check for 75 cents, saying as he handed it over, 'This includes a small gratuity for your fine service.'"

Minnesota's state universities remained of special interest to Hammel. Through his work, he gained many friends in higher education who later proved to be important contacts for the company.

CHAPTER III

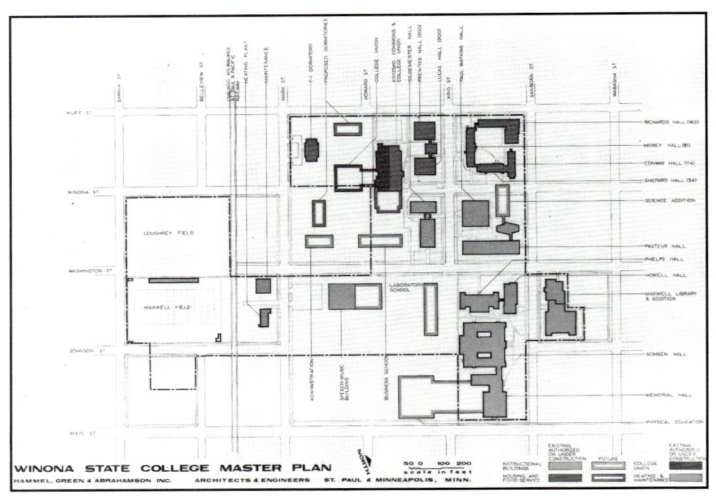
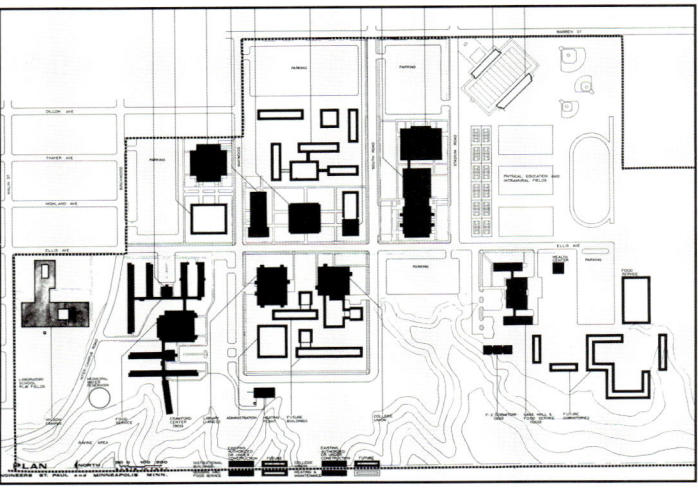
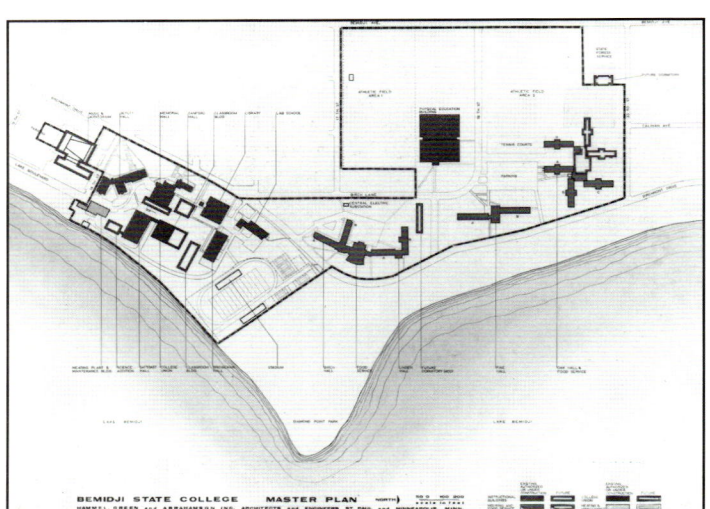
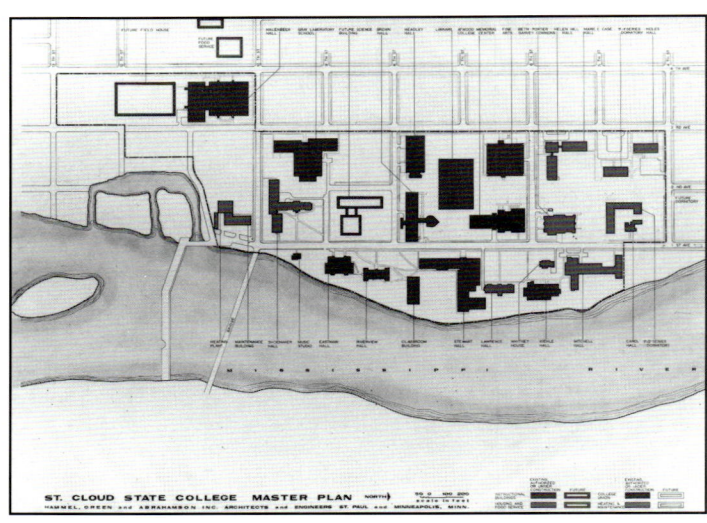
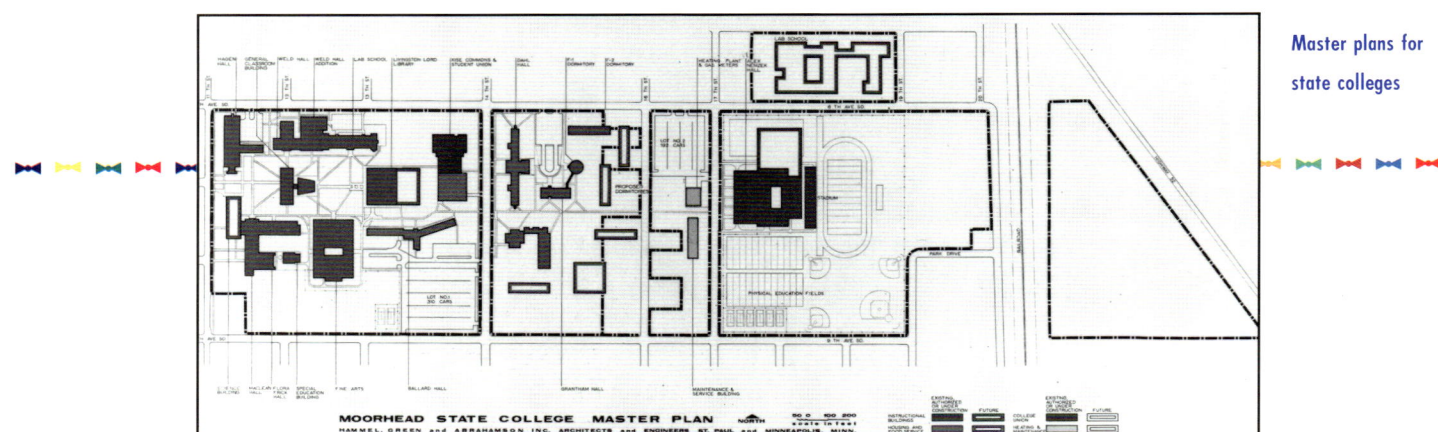

Master plans for state colleges

CHAPTER III

Dick Babcock

University of Minnesota

Since all three principals were graduates of the U of M School of Architecture, they had high hopes of getting some work from their alma mater. First they had to establish a track record. By 1956 the firm was ready. Hammel and Green, Inc. heard about the University's need for a crop research building and were advised to call on Dr. Charles Mayo, then a member of the Board of Regents. (At that time, the University selected its own architects.)

Not expecting that the interview in Rochester would last more than 45 minutes, Green brought along his wife so she could visit a friend. However, Dr. Mayo spent the entire afternoon with the two young architects. "We were amazed that he would spend that much time with us. He showed us through the whole Mayo Clinic, then took us to his home. He was very pleasant and exceptionally interested in architecture and in some of our ideas," recalled Green. That year they got the commission for the Crop Research Building, and began work on the project in 1957.

By that time, Richard Babcock, another U of M graduate, had joined the staff. Because of his technical orientation, Babcock was assigned to work with principal Abrahamson on the project. "The University wanted climate-controlled rooms, a relatively new concept then, to grow plants under artificial conditions that imitated a natural growing environment," said Babcock. The original design for the building on the St. Paul campus called for a glass curtain wall, but because that exceeded the budget, the wall had to be done in brick. The Crop Research Building was only the second such installation in the country at that time. Through his careful analytical work, Babcock quickly established himself as a technical design leader who excelled in detailing and working out new solutions to construction problems.

Crop Research Building, U of M, St. Paul

"Babcock was the ultimate technical person who knew the logistics of building."
Dan Swedberg

"The most important thing in life is not to accomplish for oneself alone, but for each to carry his share of collective responsibility."
William J. and Charles H. Mayo

HAMMEL GREEN AND ABRAHAMSON

CHAPTER III

Ted Butler

A typical office Christmas party of the 1960s in the Hubbard Building.

Business Struggles

Other key people joined the firm in the late 1950s, contributing substantially to the firm's success. Viona "Vi" Rice, hired in 1958 as the first full-time bookkeeper, advanced to comptroller by the mid-1970s. Architects Ron Haase, Brian Morgan, and Charles Thomsen started in 1959. Two future officers were also hired then: Jerrald "Jerry" Olson and Theodore "Ted" Butler in 1960.

With Hammel and Green's incorporation in the spring of 1956, the Board of Directors took on the responsibility of setting policy, making many administrative decisions about salaries, vacations, profits, hiring and firing, and most importantly, how to get work. In 1958, the Board decided to establish a profit-sharing plan for all employees.

With staff and projects increasing, it was time to move again. At the end of 1958, Hammel and Green, Inc. took larger quarters at 2650 University Avenue in St. Paul, across from KSTP. The move cost about $17,500, a big expense for the young firm, and by March 1960, Hammel stressed that the company's financial situation was growing critical. It must acquire bigger projects. In June, a financial consultant was brought in to help determine the best capital structure and how to achieve it. One year later, the firm had definitely improved its financial status.

The staff of about 35 now often put in long hours. To relieve the stress, various team leaders suggested "a little refreshment" be served at the end of a particularly tough week, on the last day of a person's employment, or to celebrate a new commission. These "seminars", which started about the fall of 1960 and grew into a late-Friday-afternoon tradition, became more hilarious as the staff grew. Relishing pranks, the staff members celebrated the arrival of new architectural challenges as well as their conclusions.

"They had the guts to do what other people weren't doing."
Ted Butler

HGA parties remembered

"A Family Affair...and the three who gave us running support day in, day out — Vi Rice, Mary Tighe and Linda Anderson."
Dick Babcock

CHAPTER III

The Troika

The Hubbard Building — HGA's home for many years

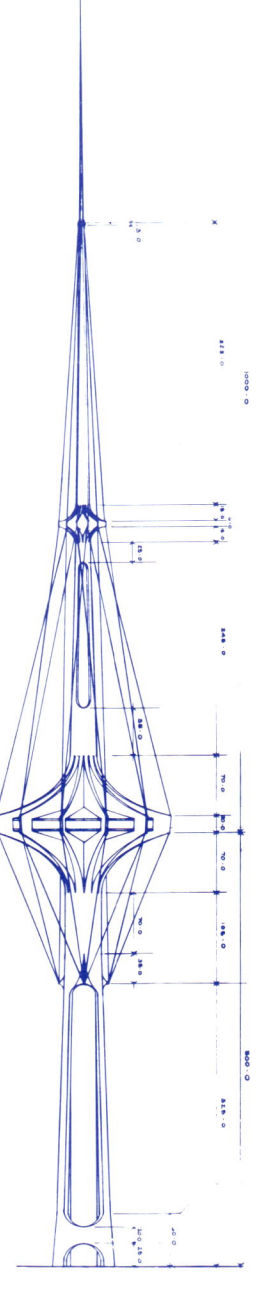

KSTP TV transmitter, restaurant, and observation tower — 1000' high.

"The Troika"

In 1961 Bruce Abrahamson became the third major stockholder. The three principals agreed that leading staff members would assume more responsibility for the firm's success if they were given the option to buy stock. Growth would provide talented people with the opportunity to achieve their potential. By 1964 stockholders included Dahlen, Peacock, Gish and Klein.

The three principals — Dick Hammel, Curt Green and Bruce Abrahamson — made all the major decisions. When they disagreed, they simply thrashed out their differences until arriving at a common point of view. For a long time, they literally ran the office, with some input from the "young turks" along the way.

From the start, Abrahamson had asserted himself as a principal designer with high standards of excellence and creativity. He spoke with a strong voice when it came to making critical business decisions, and soon after joining Hammel and Green, made it clear that he expected to have his name on the door someday. Accordingly, in June 1964 Hammel called a special stockholders' meeting. A resolution was adopted unanimously and signed by Richard Hammel and M. Lee Dahlen as amendments to the Articles of Incorporation, and on September 8, 1964, the firm's name was changed to Hammel Green and Abrahamson, Incorporated.

It was clearly understood that there was not to be "ownership" of any one position by any one member of "the troika". From that time into the 1980s, corporate offices were rotated so that the firm could benefit from the viewpoints of each of the three leaders.

With a staff of about 45, the enlarged architectural firm moved that fall into the Hubbard Building at 2675 University Avenue, where St. Paul and Minneapolis meet.

The Troika

Hammel
Pragmatic directness with simplicity and logic

Green
Delight, smaller enrichments for human scale and abundant daylight

Abrahamson
Artful organization of the whole and major impact

CHAPTER ~ IV

BETHLEHEM COVENANT CHURCH OF MINNEAPOLIS NANCY A. HOLST JOHN G. JOHNSON THERESA R. LENZMEIER LLOYD A. SEVERN DANIEL SWEDBERG RONALD C. RUSSELL WILLIAM N. SPRINGER UNITY CHURCH CARL J. REMICK BONNIE M. MITCHELL BILL KOKOTOVICH ROBERT J. CIMBURA NEDRET BUTLER LEWIS H. ROWELL RONALD T. PRITCHETTE UNIVERSITY OF MINNESOTA SCHOOL OF BUSINESS JAMES J. WENGLER JOSEPH R. WOLFSON KATHRYN R. HANSON GERALD N. LUDWIG LAWRENCE D. OLSON JANICE M. KENDLE MICHAEL MCCARTHY UNITED NATIONS SCHOOL CHARLES D. MILLER DAR  LENE BYLANDER KENNETH A. HENICK M. TERRY LARKIN DANIEL AVCHEN MICHAEL MCFOGGEN JILL GREEN URBAN DEVELOPMENT CORPORATION KEVIN J. RONNING BRUCE A. PARKER JEFFERY JOHNSON JAMES MOFFAT BRUCE PARKER KURTIS DALE JOHN POTTERTON OPERATION HEADSTART SHEILA KITZ MARVIN JOHNSON JOHN FROST RONALD HITZEMANN MARY WILSON JOSEPH EGYHAZI MARY E. WISLON UNITED STATES OFFICE OF EDUCATION LEANN R. VAN DORSTEN CHRISTOPHER COLBY RONALD SYVERSON ROBERT LUNDGREN NELESH CHOKSHI DENNIS LESLIE CARL KRAUSE JEWISH CHILD CARE ASSOCIATION AMY FILICE BRIAN BURKE JAMES DANIELSON ROGERS GEORGE ROBERT KACZKE BRUCE JILK CYNTHIA RIEBE NEW YORK PUBLIC LIBRARY KENNETH WINDEN JEFFREY JOHNSON LINDA LOKEN UDO WEGMANN CRAIG HINRICHS WALLACE SHARP RICHARD CAMPBELL RYE COUNTRY DAY SCHOOL LOREN AHLES BRYAN GATZLAFF ALEX GINTNER DORIS WELK SCOTT GALBRAITH KENNETH LEDOUX DARLENE SCHMIDT TEMPLE ISRAEL JUAN STOLESON MICHAEL MELMAN LARRY STULC GEORGE RICHES DONALD STOCK MICHAEL PEDERSON BERENICE MOHLIN LITTLE RED SCHOOLHOUSE MARLO JOHANSON JOHN BERGSTROM VLADIMIR CHAHOVSKOY BRIAN NOWAK DANIEL LARSON DEBRA ELDRIDGE BRUCE JOHNSON EAST HARLEM PRESCHOOL RONALD CARLSON GARY REETZ JOEL ANDERSON RAQUEL RUDQUIST CHRISTOPHER DIETRICH DOUG GUSARSON JOHN JUSTUS BLOCK SCHOOL

The St. Cloud Daily Times 28 November 1962

CHAPTER IV

The Benedicta Fine Arts Center, completed in fall 1964, won the firm national publicity in the cover story of the December issue of *Architectural Record* and also brought an honorable mention in the 1964 competition of the MSAIA. For 26 years, the building has been a rich resource for pursuit of the arts by both the college and community.

CHAPTER IV

TURNING POINTS

By the late 1950s, architects throughout America were showing the impact of the International Style in their works, and many were carrying Modernism one step further. Harmony, order, and precision may have been the rule of the day, but there were signs of breaking away. Late Modernists began to develop bolder sculptural forms, often using reinforced concrete. Paul Rudolph's Architecture Building at Yale, Eero Saarinen's TWA terminal in New York, and Marcel Breuer's NYU lecture hall and chapel at St. John's University in Collegeville, Minnesota were just a few.

Departing from the rigors of pure Modernism, architects at Hammel and Green were developing their own style based on the legacy of early Modernists such as Le Corbusier, Aalto, and Gropius. They did not regard themselves as regionalists or as followers of Frank Lloyd Wright, but as part of the International Style. Although they admired the singular work of the leading names in architecture, the three principals remained opposed to the one-man or hero approach and committed to their original philosophy of architecture by team. From the late 1950s to the mid-1960s, they were themselves setting some trends in the midwest, especially in the institutional field, and winning awards on a regular basis.

Benedicta Arts Center makes the cover of *Architectural Record*

The Benedicta Arts Center

In 1958 the firm was awarded its first arts building commission — from the College of St. Benedict. "Due to the size and financial limitations of the college, the nuns were thinking of only one auditorium for both theater and music," said Curt Green. "But one multi-purpose hall is often unworkable for scheduling, acoustical quality, and scale of space, so we sought a flexible solution."

The Chair of the building committee was a nun of singular fortitude and imagination, Sister Firmin Escher, who headed the fine arts department. At Green's suggestion, the entire committee of four nuns accompanied him on a drive to six different states to tour twelve new art centers. After six days on the road, car fever set in, touching off gales of laughter over silly highway or restaurant signs. This was one case where the building committee really got to know its architect.

"Give me the luxuries of life and I will gladly do without the necessities."
Frank Lloyd Wright

CHAPTER IV

The auditorium at Benedicta Arts Center.

A classically designed courtyard

To answer the client's needs, Green and his design team came up with an innovative plan — a three-in-one arts center. The hub of the building was a large stage flanked on one side by a 1,000 seat auditorium and by a forum theater on the other. A movable sound-isolating wall allowed the common stage area to serve either the auditorium or the little theater. For concerts in the auditorium, the wall was covered and two stage elevators became the music stage. The one-story fine arts center also housed music studios and practice rooms, scene shops and drama rooms, and visual arts studios. A series of courtyards and passageways wove throughout the center.

At the dedication in 1964 the sisters were deeply touched, as was Green, when "The Star Spangled Banner" rang out in the new auditorium. Recalling their working relationship, Sister Firmin said, "We trusted Curt implicitly. He was honest and helpful, and highly creative at the same time." Later, before Orchestra Hall was constructed, Stanislaw Skrowaczewski, Music Director of the Minnesota Orchestra, said, "Acoustically, I think the Benedicta is almost perfect. We get a very mellow, alive tone here. If there were a way to cart it back to the Twin Cities, we would."

Rosemount School District #196

Although many Minnesota architects were building schools in the 1950s, Hammel and Green kept an eye out for new school work. When they heard about a project in Rosemount School District #196, they acted immediately. One day as Hammel and Green headed back to the Twin Cities from Austin, Minnesota, they impulsively dropped in at the Rosemount District Office to see Superintendent Lambert Baumgartner. As they were ushered in, Baumgartner said, "Oh, you're Hammel and Green? We just

"Our architecture may be shades of grey but it ages well."
Bruce Abrahamson

CHAPTER IV

hired you last night." They had not even been interviewed! That remodeling project was the beginning of a 30-year partnership with the Rosemount School District.

Saint Bede's Priory

Saint Bede's Priory, another landmark building, won the firm its first national AIA award in 1967, and brought major recognition. The jury commented: "The harmony of undisturbed nature and bold, simple, unmistakably man-made forms is this project's most rewarding and mature accomplishment."

The challenge for principal Green and project designer Ted Butler (working with ecclesiastical consultant Frank Kacmarcik) was to create a motherhouse for Benedictine sisters, and an academy for 150 girls. After walking the site with Sister Denis Smith, prioress, in 1961, Green suggested that several building masses with a free play of undulating walls, stair towers and small courts could weave pleasantly across the rolling Wisconsin hillside. The sisters agreed, and the designers went to work developing a plan of irregular informality. When the project was finished Sister Denis said, "We were thrilled to death." Both architects were also proud of the results. In later years, Green remarked, "Saint Bede's Priory became the peak of interest within my own personal achievements."

The Donaldson Company

Another project illustrating the growing importance of the engineering department was for The Donaldson Company, a manufacturer of industrial mufflers, air cleaners, and liquid purification equipment. In 1960 Hammel received a call from Frank Donaldson, president, announcing his company's intentions to move to the suburbs and asking Hammel and Green to develop a master plan for new corporate headquarters in Bloomington.

Founded in 1915, the company had reached the point where its Pelham Boulevard facilities in St. Paul had become overcrowded and noisy. On the new site, the design team had to solve the problem of isolating the administrative offices from the blasting noises emanating from factory and test areas. First, it created separate buildings for office, laboratory, and boiler house. In addition, it designed the buildings with "cavity walls" — two walls of concrete blocks with a layer of air between. Around the acoustic laboratory, engineers placed grounded copper screens in the walls to keep out radio interference. Pyramidal roof forms became the major design element of the other two buildings.

Frank Donaldson recalled, "We knew Hammel and Green had not done a commercial project as yet and felt they would break their backs to outdo themselves. They had the best educational backgrounds. Dick was a Harvard man and so am I. Best of all, Dick did not tell the customer that we had to have this or that. He was an informal person, with a great sense of humor." This was the beginning of a relationship that served as an outstanding example of how an architectural firm can make the client part of the team. The firm has since worked with The Donaldson Company for more than two decades, designing 400,000 square feet of space.

As the nation's pollution problems grew, The Donaldson Company grew too, and by 1973 it needed more space for research. Hammel Green and Abrahamson, Inc. was asked to remodel an adjacent plant for additional executive offices and a computer room. With the approach of the 1980s, the company needed even more facilities and offices. So in 1981, the architects designed an addition for the Donaldson headquarters — a multi-story research

---

"We felt they would 'break their fannies' to outdo themselves for us."
Frank Donaldson

The finished design of St. Bede's Priory gave the complex a timeless character, mindful of an Italian hillside village.

CHAPTER IV

laboratory and office building joined by an open atrium. A glass curtain wall maximized passive solar heating in winter and a series of peaked pyramidal skylights brought natural light into the offices.

Central to the success of this project was the engineering by Harry Wilcox and Robert Kaczke. A central energy plant was devised to meet all present and future heating and cooling needs. An integral part of the energy-saving design was an electric water-chilling system that stored chilled water during off-peak hours for next-day air-conditioning. This innovation eliminated the higher costs of peak-load electrical service. The scheme captured two engineering awards: in 1981, an Energy Management Award from the ASHRAE Minnesota chapter, and in 1982, a Gateway to Energy Management Award for significant energy achievement in a new industrial facility from ASHRAE, Region VI.

The St. Paul Skyway System

In 1964 Hammel Green and Abrahamson, Inc. was commissioned to design a second-level pedestrian system for St. Paul on the recommendation of the Urban Design Committee of the St. Paul Chapter of the AIA and the Housing and Redevelopment Authority. The charge was to connect 12 blocks in the "Capital Centre" downtown renewal area — a many-faceted retail, commercial, financial and residential complex — and to integrate open spaces and public plazas within the area. It was the firm's first urban center design and planning project.

After cost analyses and feasibility studies had identified the best routes and street access, the design team, working with the Housing and Redevelopment Authority, came up with St. Paul's first skyways, a totally integrated network of second-level bridges

The Donaldson Company's new corporate headquarters

Harry Wilcox

Bruce Abrahamson and Hugh Peacock hard at work

and concourses. The first skyway bridge, connecting the Pioneer Building with the Federal Courts Building, opened in 1967. Handsomely detailed, the glass-walled bridge of structural steel painted a rich dark brown was glazed with bronze plate glass (changed to clear glass for transparency in subsequent bridges). Fourteen skyway bridges of harmonious design were completed in the next three years. The firm also developed a system of directional graphics to guide pedestrians through the concourses.

Hammel Green and Abrahamson continued to expand the skyway system for St. Paul, and after additional feasibility studies in 1976, it completed more bridges linking hotels, City Hall, retail, parking, health care, and museum facilities. Design, for the most part, has remained consistent with the original so that St. Paul is unique in having a uniformly matching concourse system. "We look at it as a total pedestrian traffic plan," said principal architect

CHAPTER IV

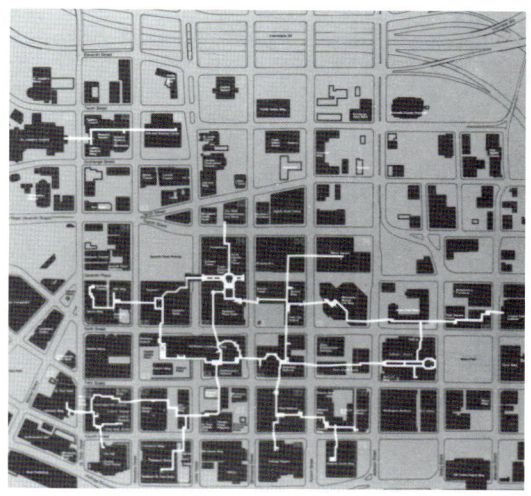

In 1968, Capital Centre won a merit award for urban design from the U.S. Department of Housing and Urban Development.

Bruce Abrahamson who worked on the project for over 20 years with project architect Perry Bolin, who joined the company in 1967. John Pearson of Johnston-Sahlman was the original structural engineer. By 1989, 32 bridges connected over three miles of skyways in St. Paul, comprising what is believed to be the largest such system in the country.

The Minneapolis Clinic of Psychiatry and Neurology

With a decade of work behind it in 1963, the firm felt confident enough to take on most any kind of architectural project. That year, doctors at the Minneapolis Clinic of Psychiatry and Neurology contacted Abrahamson about a new building. They had definite aesthetic and space requirements. The building was to be warm and inviting, take advantage of its site overlooking a small lake, yet be limited to one-and-a-half stories by height

The Minneapolis Clinic was chosen for a MSAIA Honor Award in 1967. The jury cited the building for its "human quality" and noted that "it showed great concern for the satisfaction of the patient as well as the client." A national AIA and American Medical Clinics Association award followed in 1969.

"Frustration is when your cope runneth over."
HGA Anonymous

HAMMEL GREEN AND ABRAHAMSON

CHAPTER IV

Waves in the birch reredos of Unity Church.

The Lutheran Church of the Reformation, first phase.

restrictions in Golden Valley, a Minneapolis suburb. The entrance road was well above the roof level of the proposed building, so roof design would be especially important.

With Abrahamson as principal architect, the design team came up with a non-institutional-looking building, using redwood for the exterior and many windows overlooking the lake. Other natural materials such as copper roof edges and granite boulder berms lent a residential character to an environment specially planned to put clients at ease. A series of pods were devised for the various psychiatrists' and neurologists' offices. "We wanted to preserve privacy for our clients. So in our meetings with Abrahamson, he suggested dividing the building into pods. He had innovative ideas and was cooperative and gracious in offering solutions," recalled psychiatrist Dr. Donald Daggett.

Churches of Distinction

Architects have always gloried in designing churches. Contemporary architects, while simplifying church design, still aim to create churches that uplift the human spirit. In the midwest, budgets have often been quite limited, but in the 1950s and 1960s, word reached the religious community of Hammel Green and Abrahamson's reputation in the institutional field. Personal contacts resulted in several commissions.

Unity Church

Unity Church (Unitarian) of St. Paul built a new church in 1905 of buff-colored sandstone with a red slate roof. By 1957 the congregation had outgrown the building and called on Hammel and Green to expand its facilities for religious education. Six years later, after a disastrous fire destroyed much of the original church

"Design is the art of communicating, our products are our language."
Bruce Abrahamson

HAMMEL GREEN AND ABRAHAMSON

The Unity Church narthex surrounded a new courtyard.

"Design is a process of direction and making decisions."
Dick Hammel

CHAPTER IV

and its Ames Memorial Chapel, the firm was given the task of restoring it. Through patient work with the building committee, principal architect Hammel and his team succeeded in preserving the qualities of the original church. In January 1965 the newly restored and expanded church was formally dedicated, with the Reverend Arthur Foote presiding. In the remodeled church, the architects retained the old wooden beams, replaced the dark paneling with white plaster, and transformed the hole in the roof into a graceful skylight. To heighten the vertical, Hammel introduced a handsome birch reredos behind the pulpit. Later Ray McGee, Chairman of the church's Board of Trustees, wrote: "Mr. Hammel redesigned Unity in light. The 'veil of mystery' undulating in waves of natural wood was his greatest gift to us."

Lutheran Church of the Reformation

Although Hammel and Green's first church was an addition for Bethlehem Covenant Church of Minneapolis, its first major new religious work was the Lutheran Church of the Reformation in St. Louis Park. The simple, economically constructed church was built in two stages. It won a MSAIA Merit Award in 1959, and again after expansion in 1972. A dramatic barrel-vaulted roof gave it distinction. In 1970 the church became the latest model for flexibility within a liturgically oriented space, accommodating religious, theatrical, and music programs with ease.

U of M School of Business Administration

Discussions about expanding the U of M campus began in the early 1950s, and by 1954 land had been acquired on the west bank of the Mississippi. In 1960 the U of M hired three East Coast architects to work with its own architect, Winston Close; and three local firms — Hammel and Green, Cerny Associates, and Magney, Tusler, Setter, Leach and Lindstrom. As project architect Dick Babcock recalled, "We did the School of Business Administration, the Cerny office did the tower, and Setter Leach took on the classroom building. It was quite a committee design effort." Hugh Peacock represented Hammel and Green as consultant and Bruce Abrahamson led the planning.

From the start, the U of M and the designers agreed the new campus should be as compressed as possible. Three classroom buildings were completed in 1962. For Hammel and Green, this was the second project in what would become a long-standing relationship with the U of M.

The Lutheran Church of the Reformation, second phase.

CHAPTER ~ V

Brian gatzlaff Robert jepsen William poppert John anderson Randi compere Thomas johnson Ted davis Cloquet senior high school Rene poradek Nancy stark Richard brownlee James husnik Marvin johnson Robert krueger Harry mallgrave Hopkins school district #274 Kathryn taaffe James coleman Horhon chu Kathy wickham Martha thomson James butler Richard carlson School district #277 Leslie goossens Alex newcomer Maureen bellows Colleen fretschel Mark whalley David jansen Peter knaeble School district #197 Robert nielsen David goossens Daniel kallenbach Mary maietta Warren kokes Leigh rolfshus Gary olafson Marguerite ball Julianne snow Sue wadsworth Pat barry Sandy christie Greg huonder Pat carroll Martha yunker University of l'aquila Richard heise John lavander Bruce holt Peter graffunder Dana daniels Thomas lillyman Ramy gill Gustavus adolphus college Cathy andrews Richard christensen Michael joyce Paul aasgaard George bloom Joesph desrosier Donald arneson College of saint catherine Sue delaney Anne paper Roger quick Greg haley Jane strovas Mark dohrmann John panian Hamline university Reza mehralian Sally daniels Janice heinig Ronald oblekson Robert cunningham George hutchinson Cindy le tourneau University of minnesota health sciences Debra sanders John strachota Reneé benusa Laura poucher Robin reid Shelly lofgren William huntress Becketwood cooperative Kathy nelson David janous Stephen leighty Greg huonder Stephen leighty Lawrence burfiend Stefan helgeson Presbyterian homes of minnesota Michael roach John titus Leigh rolfshus James mosher Mark cotroneo Thomas hunt Dayna dorle Saint therese of hopkins Bill o'malley Tim sessions Liz bertz Milo pinkerton Ronald mccoy Christine james Lynda kamps Rosemount school district #196 Keith anderson Tim anderson

CHAPTER V

GROWING PAINS

Ron Haase

The innovative East Harlem Preschool won a *Progressive Architecture* award in 1971 for HGA's New York office.

American architecture in the mid-1960s became looser and more free-flowing. Many distinguished architects made their mark — Eero Saarinen with his innovative Dulles Airport near Washington, D.C. and towering black granite CBS Building in New York; Philip Johnson, who turned to decorative classicism with the Carter Museum in Fort Worth and the New York State Theater; Louis Kahn for his Kimball Art Museum in Fort Worth; Paul Rudolph for his sculptural use of striated concrete in the Endo Laboratories in Garden City, New York; and I. M. Pei for geometrical structures like the MIT Earth Sciences Tower. No wonder, in such a heady atmosphere, that the three principals of Hammel Green and Abrahamson often talked about reaching beyond the midwest towards a national practice.

Opening a New York Office

One of the young architects on the staff between 1959 and 1964 was U of M graduate Ron Haase. He "cut his teeth" working on school design with Dick Hammel, Bruce Abrahamson, and Curt Green, so it was no surprise when the Ford Foundation's Educational Facilities Laboratories in New York asked him to become staff designer for school and college planning. He left the St. Paul firm in 1964, and for two years, worked with some of the nation's exceptional educators.

Seeing architectural opportunity in these connections, Haase contacted his former mentors to suggest they might mutually benefit by opening a New York office. "I was delighted that they responded favorably," recalled Haase, "and in a few months, we found space near the United Nations building." At first, the work there was research-oriented — consulting for the United Nations School, the Urban Development Corporation for all new schools on Roosevelt Island, Operation Headstart, and the U.S. Office of Education.

When the practice grew, the branch moved to larger quarters in lower Manhattan where its staff converted a manufacturing loft into a no-frills, flexible office space. By 1967, clients included the Jewish Child Care Association, the New York Public Library System, Rye Country Day School, Temple Israel in Great Neck, Long Island, and the Little Red Schoolhouse, Greenwich Village.

Christmas, 1968 — St. Paul office sends darts to Minneapolis office. Minneapolis gives St. Paul a dart board photo.

Christmas, 1969 — St. Paul office gives Minneapolis a photo of the dart board in the bottom of a bird cage housing a love bird.

New York City telephone directory as of June 16, 1989 listed 212-687-2647 for HGA's branch office (closed in 1971!)

CHAPTER V

By 1970 the New York office had obtained a challenging project from the New York City Board of Education for the East Harlem Preschool and the Block School. In this social experiment, both schools were to serve as neighborhood centers for the enrichment of preschoolers' educational, cultural, and social experience. Haase and his project designer, Clark Neuringer, devised an innovative solution: By renovating an abandoned supermarket and leasing space from a synagogue, they developed a playful, free space varying from open, high-ceilinged areas with tiled floors to carpeted, tucked-away alcoves. For the effort, they won a *Progressive Architecture* design award in 1971.

Most of the firm's New York clients were in education, and when recession hit, numerous bond issues and fund-raising efforts failed; the effect of the funding cuts was disastrous. Ironically, in 1971, the same year the New York office won its first award, Hammel Green and Abrahamson was forced to close it. Haase continued in education, first at Franconia College in New Hampshire, and later at the University of Florida.

Staff Expansion of the Mid-1960s

As the nation's economy expanded in the mid-1960s and the demand for new construction grew, the company's financial performance improved. Major staff expansion became necessary. Abrahamson, who continued to teach part-time at the U of M School of Architecture, filled staff needs with the best and the brightest young graduates. Some of his former students who joined the firm then were: Wesley Sorensen in 1959, Duane Blanchard and Eldon Burow in 1965, Michael Niemeyer and Jerry Olson in 1966, William Anderson in 1967, Kurt Rogness and Dan Swedberg in 1969, and Dan Avchen in 1972. All eventually became stockholders as did four key engineers hired in the 1960s: Kenneth Schultz in 1964, Harry Wilcox in 1965, Robert Parupsky in 1967, and James Goulet in 1968. Another future stockholder hired then was Rodney Erickson, for specifications, in 1964.

The main office was still in the Hubbard Building in St. Paul although a small Minneapolis office was maintained in the Wesley Temple Building from 1963 to 1967. Since the architects were officed right next door to KSTP Radio and Television, a neighborly camaraderie developed, and with it, several remodeling projects and additions. The first was a large audience-participation studio with a public lobby entrance. Several years later a glass-enclosed, two-level link with the Hubbard Building, housing executive offices, new studios for KSTP-FM, and a high-tech newsroom for KSTP Television, was added. Principal Hammel, with project architect Bill Anderson, came to know the station's founder, Stanley E. Hubbard, Sr., well enough to anticipate his requests. Blustery though the senior Hubbard was, Hammel always admired his pioneering spirit and resolute determination to excel.

While the firm practiced in the Hubbard Building, the office atmosphere was still informal. Everyone pitched in to handle the workload. Mary Tighe recalled that the staff didn't even take holidays when pressure was on to get a project out. Lee Dahlen, then manager of operations, also remembered long hours. Informal holiday parties became annual affairs anticipated by everyone. Usually one of the design teams created a slide show to regale the crowd; food was cooked by the staff. Linda Anderson, longtime administrative assistant who joined the staff in 1964, recalled how "everyone helped put on the party, but they sure disappeared fast at clean-up time!"

> "Here where we have all the disciplines, we're more or less equals with the architects. The engineer can impose, not dominate the situation."
> Jim Goulet

CHAPTER V

Four Big High Schools

Back on the job, design excellence was paying off for the company. By the late 1960s, the firm had established itself as a big-league player in the design of educational facilities, so much so that four major high school projects came into the office at one time. Cloquet, on Minnesota's Iron Range, the first project commissioned in 1965, was quickly followed by three other Twin Cities area high schools — Hopkins-Lindbergh, Mound-Westonka, and Henry Sibley in West Saint Paul.

Mound Westonka dedicated its new high school in October 1971, and the following year its design won a MSAIA Merit Award.

A striking feature of the new Hopkins Lindbergh Senior High School was the two-story student mall, accented with bright colors in super graphics, with two levels of departments grouped around it. In 1973, the design won a MSAIA Merit Award for HGA.

Because the Henry Sibley High School, dedicated in 1971, had to be extra large in scale, the architects designed it as three schools under one roof.

In May 1969, Senator Hubert H. Humphrey made the dedication address at Cloquet Senior High School.

Mound Westonka High School

CHAPTER V

Cloquet Senior High School

With Hammel and Butler leading the Cloquet High School design team, the architects tackled the problem of how to build a senior high in the middle of a tree farm on a rolling site. The school district wanted a building that fit the environment and expressed the character of the town known as "wood city."

"We planned a two-level school so we could save the trees, lots of beautiful evergreens and maples," said Butler. "Then we divided the school into several units to reduce the scale and give it a campus-like feeling." Initially the building was programmed for a traditional educational plan, but as interest grew in the new, more flexible modular scheduling system, the architects adjusted the plan. In 1967 the school won a citation from the American Association of School Administrators.

Hopkins Lindbergh Senior High School

The growth of the western suburbs necessitated a need for a second high school for Hopkins School District #274. It had to accommodate 1,500 students (expandable to 1,900) and allow for flexible scheduling, new teaching media, resource centers, and a variety of other needs. For the design solution, principal architect Abrahamson and project architect Bill Anderson proposed an educational mall concept that immediately appealed to teachers and administrative staff. In this plan, all departmental spaces were organized around a central resource center.

Six months of concentrated effort went into the programming phase, during which the architects worked closely with the Hopkins School Board, administration, and teaching staff. The result, in spring of 1971, was in many ways a forerunner of contemporary educational facilities.

Mound Westonka High School

As the 1960s came to an end, Mound, a suburban community in the Lake Minnetonka area, and School District #277 needed a high school for 1,200 students (expandable to 2,000) on 45 acres of gently rolling land. The school board's list of requirements included large areas for cars and buses, physical education fields, a swimming pool with spectator seating, and most important, adaptable space for flexible, modular scheduling using team-teaching, with individual identity for academic departments.

Working closely with the administration, the design team came up with a distinctive high school, tailor-made to the community's needs. Within one two-story concrete building, the architects assembled departmentalized groups of units. Each department was oriented toward a common circulation spine, providing multi-purpose use of circulation spaces. Hammel and Butler, working with project manager Eldon Burow and architect Dan Swedberg, called it "the street" within a school.

Henry Sibley High School

Of four high school projects tackled by the firm between 1968 and 1970, Henry Sibley in West St. Paul was by far the largest. Sprawling School District #197, which had never had a high school, desperately needed space for a projected 3,200 students. After much discussion, the decision was made to build one big school on 80 acres of sloping land with a panoramic view.

Because the building had to be larger than most high schools, the architects designed three schools under one roof, each independent but with some spaces common to all. Each, for example, had access to a central instructional materials center (IMC). The concept of "home schools" helped give the tenth,

---

"I'd rather be good than different."
Mies van der Rohe

CHAPTER V

eleventh, and twelfth graders a clear sense of group identity. Separate dining spaces overlooking the countryside were a welcome feature.

The first stage of Henry Sibley High School, accommodating about two-thirds of its final capacity, was dedicated in September 1971. Its design solution reflected educational trends in secondary education — greater emphasis on individual initiative, educational flexibility, and an increased variety of learning spaces.

What did all these high schools have in common? "Each was unique; they had to be to meet the needs of each client," said Green. Also, Green recalled, the high school projects helped see the firm through the recession. When he was company treasurer in 1971, banks were short of money. Payments for services on schools enabled the firm to take on the highly unusual role of lending $200,000 to First National Bank of St. Paul.

Higher Education

All kinds of educators called on the company's expertise during the 1960s. A small but unique laboratory project for the U of M in 1963 particularly intrigued Hammel, who had an abiding interest in science and especially in what was then a new scientific area, chronobiology. Working closely with Franz Halberg, who pioneered in this field at the university, the architect conceived a cost-effective way of remodeling the periodicity analysis laboratories by redesigning Lyon Lab into large rooms with many working places, saving the cost of walls and doors. "My colleagues and I were deeply grateful that Dick gave time and competent advice far beyond the scope of his university contract," recalled Halberg, who became internationally known for his work. Later, Hammel reworked the design for a leading European laboratory in chronobiology at the University of L'Aquila, Italy.

Kolthoff Hall — The new addition to the Chemistry Building included four columns which met the demands of U of M President Wilson.

CHAPTER V

U of M Chemistry Building

In 1965, the firm was commissioned by the U of M to design an addition for the Chemistry Building on the Northrop Mall. Project architect Dick Babcock, principal Abrahamson, and mechanical engineer Ken Schultz worked closely with Stewart Fenton, Chair of the Chemistry Department, and Paul O'Connor to resolve the design. They faced a real challenge: to complete the U of M mall in the spirit of Cass Gilbert's 1908 design, including four monumental columns. Opposed to non-functional monumentalism, this posed a problem for the architects. Abrahamson tried a compromise with University President O. Meredith Wilson, but Wilson argued that traditional columns, necessary or not, should be carried through on the mall. The result was that exterior columns were added to the facade as echoes of the other mall buildings.

The chemistry building addition was Hammel Green and Abrahamson's first systems building with a mechanical shaft space through the full height of the structure. This vertical utility space plus a modular layout enabled the U of M to adjust its state-of-the-art labs to constantly changing needs. As the labs generated almost every known type of chemical contaminant, company engineers used over a hundred fume hoods to extract gaseous wastes.

Gustavus Adolphus College, Fine Arts Complex

Gustavus Adolphus, a popular private college in St. Peter, Minnesota, wanted to reflect its Swedish heritage and memorialize opera star Jussi Bjorling in a facility housing the visual arts, music, and drama departments. So when the firm was interviewed for the project, it was fitting that Curt Green, who had designed two other

A new chemistry lab at Kolthoff Hall

"We found a catalog that illustrated gargoyles as a standard product. They were used as small elements of "fun" fulfilling our charge to "design Scandinavian — influenced architecture to be enjoyed," wrote Curt Green.

"There were times in the '60s when construction got held up because of the student demonstrations."
Dick Babcock

CHAPTER V

Curt Green visits with Anna-Lisa Bjorling (widow of opera star Jussi Bjorling) and Lennart Nylander, Swedish Ambassador to the U.S.

leading art centers, represented the company and became principal architect and designer when HGA received the commission.

The resulting L-shaped complex contained two buildings — one for visual arts, the other for performing arts. In the visual arts sector were galleries, lecture rooms, and art studios lit with north light from clerestory windows. The performing arts wing was divided into two sections — music and drama. Within the music department was the 450-seat Jussi Bjorling Memorial Hall, named in honor of the opera star whose friend, Robert Merrill, performed at the 1971 dedication. The drama department included the 300-seat Anderson Memorial Theater with thrust stage for student use.

The College of St. Catherine

When the Minnesota Orchestra played its first concert in its new St. Paul home in I. A. O'Shaughnessy Auditorium, Music Director Stanislaw Skrowaczewski and College President Alberta Huber, CSJ, took many bows before an elated audience. An excited Green represented Hammel Green and Abrahamson at the celebration. At last the orchestra had a prestigious home in St. Paul and the College had a new performing arts center. With its five-story exterior facade of boldly formed concrete, the new hall became a sculptural landmark on this urban campus.

Carl Nyrén of Stockholm provided a Swedish influence for the Gustavus Adolphus arts complex.

Structural engineering for the project was designed by Milan Johnston of Johnston-Sahlman. In the 1960s, Johnston had distinguished himself working with poured concrete for Marcel Breuer's famous St. John's University Chapel and Library. In recalling O'Shaughnessy, Johnston remarked, "Curt had a tremendous reputation with the client. O'Shaughnessy is done in a lot more delicate way than Breuer's work."

> "All great buildings are inescapably of their own moment in time; they are the signposts of civilization. They become 'timeless' in relation to their greatness — later."
> Ada Louise Huxtable

CHAPTER V

The challenge for the architects was designing an all-purpose auditorium yet intimate theater in one space. With the help of special consultants George Izenour and Bolt, Beranek and Newman, the design team (principal Green, working with Robert Takaichi) came up with an innovative solution. Total seating was 1,800, but the movable ceiling made it possible to close off a balcony for 1,100, leaving a 700-seat theater on the main floor. "Mr. Green was very careful while working with us to create a building that grew out of the life of our institution," said Sister Alberta.

The firm (with Roger Freeberg as designer) also designed a visual arts building featuring distinctive, sloped window-wall studios. With northern light a key to the design, the Arts Building expressed the wishes of students and faculty for a pleasant work/study space and also won a MSAIA Honor Award in 1971.

Hamline University: Bush Memorial Library

Another award-winning project was the new library for Hamline University. Following a master plan study, the design team created a flexible brick and concrete block building, complete with a pedestrian linking system and friendly interior spaces. For the library interior, project architect James Sorenson selected contemporary furnishings of fine woods upholstered in rich dark purples and reds. When dedicated in 1971 by Bush Foundation President Elmer L. Andersen, the library was eight times the size of the old one. Richard P. Bailey, President of Hamline, and Hammel established a camaraderie that encouraged Hammel to present him with a special gift at the 1971 dedication — the first sketches of "Bailey Memorial Hall." Hammel said with an impish grin, "We have already notified the development director to obtain enough trading stamps to pay for it."

O'Shaughnessy Auditorium, named for a well-known local philanthropist, won a 1971 MSAIA Honor Award with the jury announcing, "This is a very handsome, well-detailed solution to a highly complex problem; it is a beautiful and highly utilitarian building that announces itself and its function boldly on the campus."

On dedication day in the fall of 1971, Hamline President Richard P. Bailey accepted a symbolic key to Bush Memorial Library from Bush Foundation President Elmer L. Anderson while George Peterson, President of Hamline's Board, looked on.

"Consistency is a real hallmark of HGA."
Gary Reetz

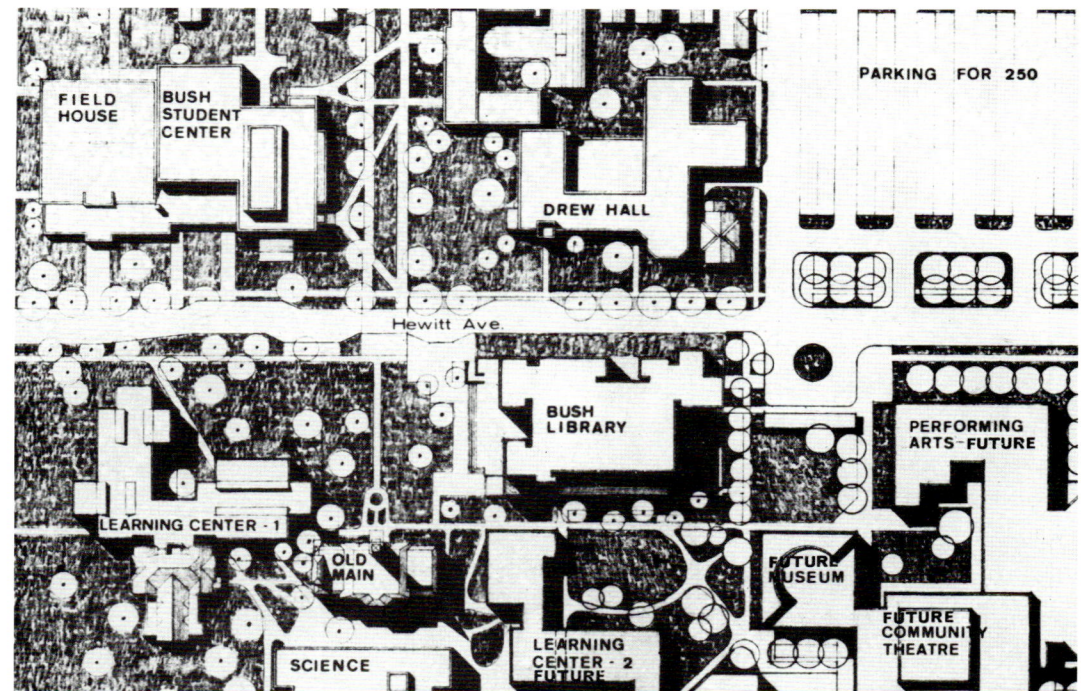

Master plan for Hamline University

In both design and concept, the Paul H. Giddens Alumni Learning Center at Hamline University took honors in the 1972 MSAIA competition.

CHAPTER V

Paul H. Giddens Alumni Learning Center

Old Main was the place where learning had begun on the Hamline University campus in the 1880s. With historic preservation in mind, the Board Members challenged the architects to save the 1900 library structure and give them a totally modern learning center at the same time. After thorough study, project architect Bill Anderson, principal Hammel, and the design team came up with a refreshing way to link the old building with the new, relating the existing building through form and materials. The original stone-columned entrance was retained as a facade within the new lobby. With a vaulted, coffered ceiling surrounding the old pediment, the entrance lent dignity and tradition to the new space. Included in the new learning center were open labs, classrooms, work areas, faculty offices, and seminar rooms looking out on the campus.

Hamline University School of Law

The next architectural challenge from this liberal arts institution was a new law school on a site defining the southern border of the campus. Founded independently, Hamline's School of Law merged with Hamline University in 1976, making it the only private-university-affiliated law school in the upper midwest.

The designers sited the main entrance at the terrace level of Bush Memorial Library, so the two structures could share a garden courtyard. They also visually related the new law school to the library with a dominating concrete screen, giving symbolic emphasis to the entrance, moot court, and law library. For the interior, they organized the building around a three-story skylit linear atrium. The entire building was energy efficient.

Still another project for the College was the addition of a 300-seat theater to the existing Fine Arts Building. With the completion of the theater addition in 1982, Hammel Green and Abrahamson had served Hamline University for almost a decade. A close working relationship with the Board and administrative staff, nurtured by Hammel and Bill Anderson, provided continuity and consistency with the original master plan.

The First Joint Venture — U of M Health Sciences

The company took on its first joint venture in 1968, and it was a big one. After a national search, the U of M hired The Architects Collaborative (TAC) of Cambridge to do a long-range expansion plan for the health sciences. The U of M then selected four local firms to work with TAC: The Cerny Associates; Ellerbe; Hammel Green and Abrahamson; and Setter Leach and Lindstrom. Subsequently Ellerbe withdrew, and the remaining three firms formed a separate corporation, Health Sciences Architects &

The Hamline University School of Law brought yet another MSAIA Honor Award in 1981.

"Too bad all our buildings can't be built indoors."
Dick Hammel

CHAPTER V

Engineers (HSAE). Former Hammel and Green stockholder Hugh Peacock was the U of M architect.

Under TAC's leadership, the master plan for this 1½-million square foot project resulted in a unique building system that permitted flexible expansion on a tight urban site. It was a tremendous challenge to develop such a large building complex for construction in stages as each program was funded.

Flexibility and adaptability were the prime objectives of the architects and engineers. "Since the needs of health sciences keep changing on a regular basis, we developed a flexible approach for the interior design," said managing principal Duane Blanchard. Rather than designing separate buildings for each major function (offices, classrooms, clinics, and labs), the architects developed a modular building system that could be readily adapted for various needs.

The focal point and prototype for the other program components was the School of Dentistry, Unit A, a 19-story, 675,000 square foot building of precast concrete designed for both vertical and horizontal expansion. State-of-the-art mechanical and electrical systems were the prime responsibility of engineers Ken Schultz and Dave Martin in 1973, followed by Harry Wilcox and Gary Hall in 1974. James Goulet directed civil engineering from the outset.

Hammel Green and Abrahamson set up a special team for the Health Sciences project, even sending Blanchard and Olson to Boston in 1969 to work with the TAC design team. Architect Kurt Rogness, fresh from the MIT master's program, also worked with them. In 1974, he returned home to Minnesota to accept a new post with the firm.

As working drawings for Unit A were finalized over the next year, Unit B/C was being designed. These facilities housed the

Joint ventures are like marriage. The first office romance that became a joint venture was secretary Shirley Norling marrying architect Dave Nordale. His 1956 classy T-Bird was the envy of many.

The U of M Health Sciences complex wound up about the same size as the IDS Center in Minneapolis, with vastly more complex interior spaces. Unit A alone houses the School of Dentistry, teaching space, medical research labs, dental research labs, and animal research facilities.

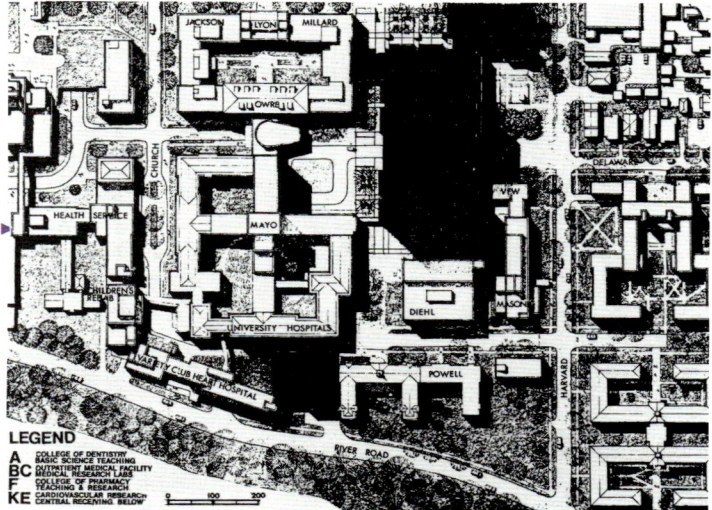

CHAPTER V

Duane Blanchard, Jerrald Olson

Hospital's outpatient clinics and medical research labs. With economic recession settling in around 1972, funding for new projects became scarce, and it was only through the efforts of Dr. Lyle French, Chair of the Health Sciences Division, and Senator Hubert Humphrey that Unit B/C was finally financed in 1974 and completed in 1978. Meanwhile, the Health Sciences design team continued work on Unit K/E, a six-level project housing cardiovascular research labs and the materials management center. This building was completed in the fall of 1975.

With four major architectural firms involved on a project of such massive scale, efficient management was critical. In 1974, the firm became concerned about leadership of the joint venture, differences of opinion among the three firms, and its own relationship with TAC. "That's when Hammel got involved. We needed someone very strong to deal with the internal politics. Dick was

Gearing up for Health Sciences

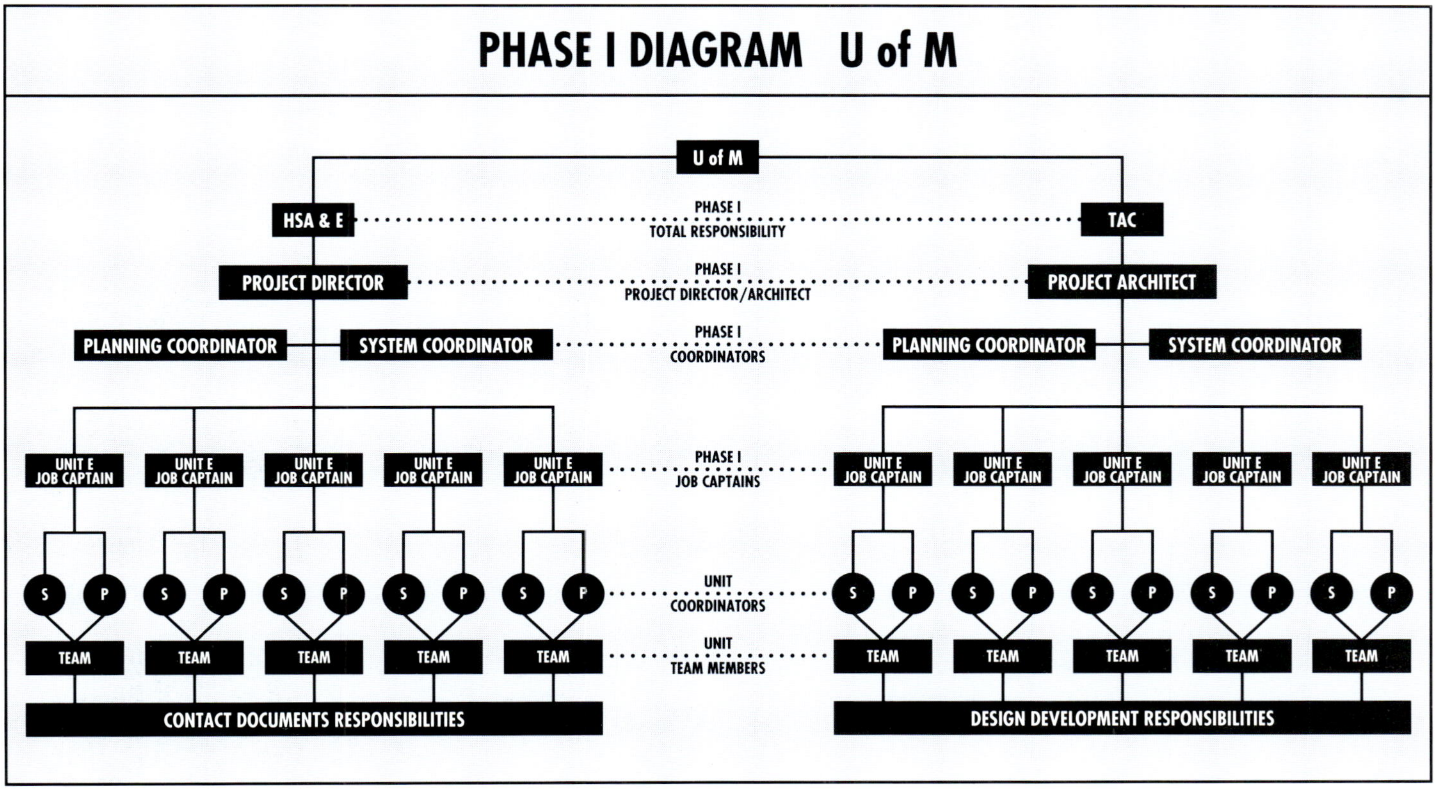

PHASE I DIAGRAM U of M

CHAPTER V

that someone," recalled Blanchard. A new office location was found, independent of the three firms, near the project site. A management team of one individual from each firm was established to manage the joint venture office.

The HSAE joint venture continued until March 1977 when Setter Leach and Lindstrom and The Cerny Associates withdrew; HSAE became a wholly-owned subsidiary of Hammel Green and Abrahamson, Inc. In September 1977, HSAE entered two joint-venture agreements with TAC — one for the redesign of Unit F and one for the development of Unit B/C shell space.

The final component of the expansion, Unit F funded in 1977, was designed three times as program requirements continued to change. Ultimately, Unit F included both the College of Pharmacy and School of Nursing. Rogness provided design leadership and Blanchard managed the effort for Hammel Green and Abrahamson (by this time known as HGA), working with TAC. This arrangement continued until February 1986 when HSAE merged into Hammel Green and Abrahamson. HGA still provides architectural and engineering services for the remaining Unit B/C shell space. Through 20 years of ups and downs, the firm has maintained continual involvement with at least 50 staff members steadily contributing to its progress. To them, Health Sciences was so challenging, so complex, so dependent on various stages of governmental funding that completing it in two decades has been a real accomplishment. "We had stepped into major health care work, and it vaulted us into a large office," said Abrahamson.

Kurt Rogness

The U of M Health Sciences complex — 20 years of continuing work

CHAPTER ~ VI

Bill beck Mike hangge Mike renstrom Dennis solberg Linda bank Saint joseph's hospital Wendel chamberlin Scott newland Peter schumacher Richard anderson Mordechi fishman William oostendorp Barbara simon Colonial church of edina Dwight fernandez Thomas reinen Gregg gossens Kathy evans David jones Sharyn ricehill John wolf Jody berg Orchestra hall Susan obrestad Thomas swearingen Caren gross Thomas johnson Vicky enger Chris cariveau Ronald christensen Honeywell corporation William gurstelle Paul williams Martin howard Jeremy bork Gregory anaas Michael tanner Gary johnson Gregory ewing Leslie green Corliss oliver Kathy massman Kathy gay Kathy nelson General mills James flannery Marti bruyes Dale muhlenpoh Norman koller Pat provinske Richard schrader Peder sulerud Gary nyberg Joao moreita (john) Michael granucci Neal wunderlich Phillip bourasa Karen saelens Mark t. johnson John larson Michael graves Cliff olson Sally grans David guindon Alexandria selvig (lexi) John carlson Jan grove Ted rozeboom Lisa helland Science museum of minnesota Keith nelson Glen heino Jim jurgens Jim dahlberg Gary anderson Yanak shagalov F. E. koennecke Robert roach Robert venturi Jodell gintner Todd labey Wes janz Dayna dorle Dennis wallace Gregory lyford Andrejs cers Marcie meditch Alabama space and rocket center Sharon nelson Tim rosen Dan hinrichs Dave muller Norm koller Carol becker Mary ann schultz Gail larson Charles moore Theresa hankel Jean ubl Mary walsh Kris gore Susan belford Arnold hieserich Dennis raddatz Gary benson Fort worth museum of science and history Garg zastrow John cameron John jurewicz Dave grossklaus Nicki litke Audrey hollatz Sherry becker Kevin conley Philip johnson Robert fontaine Tom soukup Mike huntington Dae min William blanski Andrew bailey Rodger skare Andy cers

CHAPTER VI

Subsidized housing for the elderly in Stillwater, Minnesota.

CHAPTER VI

STRUGGLING THROUGH THE RECESSION

Perry Bolin

Dan Swedberg

Throughout the architectural world of the United States at the start of the 1970s, there was a certain restlessness with Modernism. Architects were using exposed concrete forms and trying new geometric expressions, but no philosophical agenda like that of the early Modernists had evolved. "There was beginning to be a discomfort with the International Style," recalled Bob Lundgren, staff architect since 1976. "It was called sterile — too many glass boxes. People were searching for alternatives."

As the U.S. recession deepened, national architectural firms increasingly bid for business in Minnesota, adding to the already extensive local competition.

Typical subsidized housing projects of the 1960s.

"After 1969, our workload fell dramatically," reflected Lee Dahlen, then corporate secretary (and later secretary-treasurer and vice president). "We were riding so high, then suddenly our work subsided." In spring of 1969, the office staff peaked at about 90 employees including students; two years later, it was down to about 70, and it declined to a low of 42 in the summer of 1973. The New York office had closed in 1971. With the national birthrate declining, management foresaw a drop in school work and reasoned that the firm had to grow bigger in order to get work on a major scale; diversifying the practice was absolutely critical. The company decided to go into housing as developer as well as architect/engineer.

Dominium

To learn more about federal housing programs, Perry Bolin and Curt Green went to a low-income housing seminar at the University of Wisconsin at Madison in 1971. There they met a cocky, young student enrolled in the School of Real Estate — David Brierton, who was highly charged with energy, confidence, and ambition. The architects sensed he was the kind of man they were looking for. About three years later, after acquiring postgraduate experience, Brierton came calling on the firm.

After much discussion with Brierton about pursuing the business of primarily public-supported housing, the three principals decided in 1974 to set up a limited partnership called Dominium in which they personally invested, separate from HGA. Brierton was president, and

"Our involvement in the community goes beyond the actual projects themselves ...it's part of our broad social concern."
Dan Swedberg

CHAPTER VI

Hammel organized a Board of Directors, which included three real estate experts: William Clapp, Maurice Scroggins, and Richard Thompson. Abrahamson was principal in charge of design. Hammel, a Member of the Board, took on the position of go-between for the Board, designers, and developers.

"Dominium found a niche in the market. It specialized in government-assisted, low-income housing so there was little risk," said project architect Perry Bolin. The first project that Brierton landed was a low-income, senior citizen housing project in New Richland, Minnesota, followed by a similar job in Long Prairie, Minnesota. Then, another super-charger, Jack Safar, joined Dominium to assist Brierton in locating new business. About 13 or 14 projects followed, with Dominium bringing in between $15 and $20 million worth of work. Most of it was subsidized housing, built according to HUD standards. Developer selections were based on design and financial projections.

As work went on, government policy changed, and by 1982 the federal government had fulfilled its mission of building public housing all over the country. Because of this change, Dominium faced increased competition. Unlike HGA's management, Brierton and Safar were high risk-takers. "They did not share the same principles of service we did. Their approach was the bottom line on everything," said Abrahamson. Major differences arose between HGA's leaders and the Dominium entrepreneurs. "We didn't agree on basic philosophy," recalled Bolin, "and we could not resolve it." Eventually, the relationship dissolved. In 1982, the other investors withdrew and the HGA founders sold their interests to Brierton and Safar, who continued to operate Dominium.

In retrospect, the Dominium venture proved good experience for HGA, providing work during a crucial period and giving

Wes Sorenson

"While I was working in my yard this morning, I thought about these new schools ...how we plan them, stick them in the ground, nurture them along. Today we're here to enjoy the harvest." RFH

it entry to the housing market. The firm remained involved in housing (under Dan Swedberg's leadership) particularly in seniors independent living residences such as: Becketwood in Minneapolis, Gideon Pond in Bloomington, and St. Therese in Hopkins.

Rosemount School District #196

Through the lean years, HGA continued its work for Rosemount School District #196. From the start, Dick Hammel and Wesley Sorensen worked closely with school administrators, staff, faculty, and the District Board to forge schools that worked, that were a delight to enter, that helped the learning process, that faced the problems of children with physical and learning disabilities and those with special gifts. As the school population grew like topsy, Hammel and his team worked with a series of superin-

"Teaming is the way skilled people come together to benefit from one another. It distinguished the firm and still does. It's what attracted me to Hammel and Green in the first place. Dick and I were a team for decades."
Wes Sorensen

CHAPTER VI

Lee Drogemiller, first Principal of Valley Middle School, was an advocate of openness, even moving his desk into a space near the library. He sat right in the middle and loved every minute.

tendents, school boards, bond issues, and ever-increasing demands from the community. The huge school district encompassed Rosemount, Apple Valley, Burnsville, Eagan, Lakeville, and Coates.

At first, the schools such as Northview Elementary, Rosemount Elementary, and Rosemount Senior High were quite traditional. By 1965, however, the architects planned two non-traditional elementary schools, Westview and Southview. These schools used folding partitions for walls and a breezeway to connect the kindergarten, gymnasium, and cafeteria with the rest of the classrooms.

About this time, many top educators were becoming increasingly excited about the concept of open schools and team teaching. H. C. "Hap" Hanson was the first superintendent the firm worked with on an open school. A former teacher and principal, he

Parkview Elementary was one of the first open schools for Rosemount School District #196.

"Open Schools — a freer atmosphere."

CHAPTER VI

felt that "teachers restricted to their own classrooms had no way to share other teachers' ideas and methods. Team teaching in an open environment gave them the opportunity to mix, and they would all benefit." Hammel had seen open schools in action on the east coast, so he planned a trip with Hanson to tour more of these schools in Connecticut, Massachusetts, Nevada, California, and Colorado.

Hanson liked what he saw. "In that atmosphere of openness, teachers were always on display and had to function as teams more effectively. Inexperienced teachers learned more quickly by observing their peers," he said. "As for the children, it was easier for them to move around and learn from one another in this freer atmosphere." Everyone in the Rosemount School District agreed however, that it was important to continue to group the same age levels in one grade.

Diamond Path Elementary, Apple Valley, and Parkview Elementary, Lakeville

Diamond Path Elementary in Apple Valley and Parkview Elementary in Lakeville, opening in fall of 1970, were the first open-plan schools done by the firm in the Rosemount School District. Everything other than the gymnasium, cafeteria, and physical plant was in the open. "It was the boldest of any of the open schools we had seen," recalled Sorensen.

One of the advantages of an open school plan was the ease it gave children in using the IMC. Students could easily slip into comfortable spaces to sprawl out and read, or to perch in a little niche for special study. (The open plan has recently been modified or discarded in many communities, but ISD #196 has, in general, maintained its policy of openness.)

By 1973, a new bond issue was passed to fund five more

Apple Valley Senior High
"Athletics, Arts and Academics."

The spacious Apple Valley Senior High School, winner of a MSAIA Merit Award in 1976, with its lively IMC and semicircular theater became a showcase for the District.

Apple Valley High School

CHAPTER VI

buildings — Greenleaf, Echo Park, Thomas Lake and Cedar Park Elementary Schools, and Valley Middle School. The middle school became the first open school for sixth, seventh, and eighth-graders in the district. In 1975, HGA began work on the biggest school yet for Rosemount. The firm poured all its expertise, technology, and innovative design into Apple Valley Senior High. At the heart of the school, the design team placed a four-level IMC, open on all sides and painted in reds and yellows. Again the IMC allowed students ready access to resource materials and was surrounded by classrooms and corridors on all levels.

Of special pride and joy to Apple Valley Senior High is the theater. Designed with a thrust stage surrounded by 600 blue seats, this adaptable theater is used by both District high schools and community performing groups. No one will ever forget opening night in March 1976 when students outdid themselves in a production of *Godspell*. As junior Terry Berkely entered, singing "Prepare Ye the Way of the Lord", the audience caught its breath. Everyone knew the theater was a smashing success. Hammel, for one, applauded wildly, with tears streaming down his cheeks.

Getting into Medical Work

The company made another key decision during the recession — to go into medical work, this time in a big way. Accordingly, the first need was to hire a specialist in health care architecture, a man with expertise, leadership ability, and a strong marketing sense. Canadian-born George Riches was that man.

In one of those coincidences of history, Abrahamson, a member of the Minnesota Architectural Registration Board, met George Riches at the Board's offices in 1973. Although registered as an architect in Pennsylvania and Maryland, Riches was still required to take Minnesota licensing exams when he joined Ellerbe, Inc. in 1971. At that interview, Abrahamson was struck with Riches' natural confidence, architectural expertise, and outgoing manner. He knew that Riches had significant experience in the health care field.

George Riches

Riches, the son of hard working parents, grew up in a small blue-collar town north of Winnipeg where few ever went to college. He was an excellent student who liked to draw, and was encouraged to enter the School of Architecture at the University of Manitoba. "We were heavily into Mies. Everyone was doing those very pristine, minimalist kinds of detailing," recalled Riches. After graduating in 1955 and working as an architect in Winnipeg for two years, he moved to Regina, Saskatchewan, to join a young firm. There he became a partner and stayed for 12 years. He regularly put in long hard days, working on schools, offices, hospitals and, in typical small-office style, helped to do everything. Eventually dissatisfied with life on the prairies, he accepted a job in a medium-sized office in Pittsburgh. There, he seized an opportunity and wound up managing a sizable hospital project.

In 1971 an offer came from Ellerbe, Inc. in Minnesota, to become an associate director of their medical division. He traveled the country managing eight hospital projects in six states simultaneously, directing twenty-five architects and four project managers. He was given the chance to head the New Orleans office, but the location did not appeal to him. About this time, HGA invited him to head its new health care team.

"Right away I thought there would be opportunity in this growing firm, and the three principals had high standards in

> "The combination of aesthetics and high tech design makes the challenge of medical architecture greater than ever."
> George Riches

CHAPTER VI

architecture," recalled Riches. He joined HGA in 1974, became a full partner in 1978, and was elected to the Board of Directors in 1980. A strong believer in the team approach, he said, "It's much more effective than any other way of practicing."

An astute marketer, Riches became director of marketing, demonstrating to the office staff that he was a driving force who set standards and required organization. The principals soon recognized Riches' flair for competition and adeptness for organizing, combined in an easy-going style. He was a man to watch.

By that time, HGA had gained excellent experience in medical work. Those specialists became part of the medical team along with Riches: John Anderson, Duane Blanchard, Gary Hall, Jerry Olson, Kurt Rogness, Nancy Stark, and Harry Wilcox. The first hospital job they acquired was, according to Wilcox, a major breakthrough for the firm.

St. Joseph's Hospital

In 1975 HGA began a long association with St. Joseph's Hospital, one of St. Paul's oldest major health care providers. The hospital wanted to upgrade its facilities to better meet the needs of area residents.

First the design team, led by Riches and project manager John Anderson, developed a master program of phased construction. Then it designed a large four-story building in the heart of the St. Joseph complex, improving circulation and housing new intensive and coronary care units, emergency, and other services. The hospital continued to be a HGA client for major remodeling projects including a linear accelerator therapy unit, surgery, cardiology, computer room, birthing room, and CAT scanner unit. The scale of the St. Joseph's project gave HGA a track record and a reputation for design in the health care field.

George Riches

Typical Intensive Care Unit

St. Joseph's Hospital addition.

CHAPTER VI

The trumpet section of the Minnesota Orchestra.

Curt Green

Orchestra Hall, the Minnesota Orchestra's new home in 1974.

Colonial Church of Edina

From the beginning of the HGA partnership, the founders were dedicated to architecture that uplifted the human spirit. As the recession deepened, HGA faced serious staff reduction, so it was fortunate indeed, when Hammel got a call from Dave Griswold, Chairman of the Building Committee for Colonial Church of Edina. Housed in a Georgian red brick building, the congregation was outgrowing its space under the leadership of the Reverend Arthur Rouner. Some members of the building committee thought they simply had to have a new church; others thought an addition would suffice. Designer Ted Butler and principal Hammel started meeting with committee members to assess the congregation's needs and help them arrive at a solution. Thus began one of Hammel's most meaningful architectural experiences.

Orchestra Hall

Also in the early 1970s, Curt Green was called in to do feasibility studies for the possible renovation of the old Lyceum Theater in downtown Minneapolis as a new home for the Minneapolis Symphony (later the Minnesota Orchestra). The request came at an opportune time. Late in 1971, the Lyceum, known as the original home of the orchestra, had become available for purchase. Though the orchestra was still performing at Northrop, the Orchestral Association became excited about prospects for an acoustically improved concert hall on the old Lyceum site. To establish criteria for acoustical design, the association hired Cyril Harris, the New York acoustician who had helped plan Kennedy Center. Next it bought the land at 11th and Nicollet. By mid-1972, however, the Association's House Committee, chaired by Stephen Pflaum, had concluded that such a renovation was economically

"One of the most remarkable concert halls in the world."
New York Times music critic
Harold Schonberg

When Orchestra Hall opened in October 1974, *New York Times* music critic Harold Schonberg called it "tonally...one of the most remarkable concert halls in the world." For Green, the finished project "was particularly rewarding...not only because we envisioned the hall as part of our lives, but also because the new home of the orchestra bears the imprint of many people working together to meet a challenge."

Discussing their progress on the Orchestra Hall project were HGA project manager Jerry Olson, acoustician Cyril Harris, Orchestral Association President Donald L. Engel, and contractor Martin Thiede.

CHAPTER VI

unjustified. Excitement began to grow about building a new hall, complete with plaza, on Nicollet Mall in Minneapolis. Further study showed that a new structure could be built for about a third more than remodeling the Lyceum.

That was all the committee needed. In December 1972, HGA was hired as project architect, joining acoustician Cyril Harris, and Hardy Holzman Pfeiffer Associates of New York, associate architect responsible for design.

The firms were faced with a huge challenge — to design and build a world-class concert hall with support facilities in time for an October 1974 opening — only 500 calendar days away.

"The pressure was evident at our first meeting in December," said Green. "We had never worked together before, but all immediately responded with enthusiasm. Our mission was to create a very important building, responding to the needs of artists, audiences and the urban setting." The working relationship of the two architectural firms was not entirely harmonius, however. "It was New Yorkers irritated by Minnesotans and vice versa," Green said. Neverthless, the schedule was rigidly adhered to.

A fast-track construction method was immediately scheduled, and construction began in June 1973, with Jerry Olson as project manager for HGA. Because of the deadline, the Minnesota architects completed final drawings as the foundation work began. The hall was sited at an angle so that its size, setting, and shape would always be unique to the surrounding area. The orchestra committee agreed that to save time for design and be assured of acoustical success, they should use the general profile of the Kennedy Center concert hall in Washington, D.C. In theory and reality, Orchestra Hall became two buildings in one — a classic rectangular concert hall surrounded by support areas and lobby.

Designers Hugh Hardy and Malcolm Holzman came up with a colorful lobby, creating liveliness and excitement with exposed mechanical systems and flying bridges for people-watching.

In complete contrast was the warmly elegant concert hall. There, acoustics were what mattered. The Orchestral Association clearly stated: "Above all, the building should help achieve that most important goal, the excellence of acoustics." Acoustician Harris noted: "All materials were selected to provide optimum reverberation characteristics for symphonic music." Unique to the hall were the irregular cubes protruding from the ceiling and back of the stage, replacing the decorated cherubed ceilings of the old tradition. Hardy's ceiling was developed to its final geometry by the HGA design team. The cubes worked, and so did the acoustics!

All those who had taken part in building the landmark project were invited to a special premiere one week before the public opening. When Stanislaw Skrowaczewski lifted his baton and the orchestra responded with "The Star Spangled Banner", many in the audience were moved to tears. "I had never in my life *really* heard the majestic sounds of our very own symphony orchestra," said one audience member. For HGA construction field representative Rogers George, it was "a dream come true".

Months later, chief mechanical engineer Harry Wilcox found himself decked out in a tuxedo and sitting in the trumpet section in the middle of a performance! The musicians had insisted that he personally test a spot where they were chilled by a cold draft. This revealing experience and test data enabled HGA engineers to correct the problem (not of their own making). The Orchestra Hall project played its part in helping HGA through the recession, but Wilcox never did learn to play the trumpet.

"There never would have been a Parthenon if you had to worry about air conditioning."
Harry Wilcox

CHAPTER ~ VII

Boston's museum of science Paul evenson Gerald johnson Robert wray Jim moravek Karen caswell Jeannette jordan Mike mcgie Carol chaffee John burgee Peter duwenhoegger Dan ward Mark moeller Chris strom Martha mcinnis Vince nonnemacher Sandy parsley Carnegie science institute Diane midgett David hatton Leslie peterson Kent larson Tom schwaegerle John monnens Peter cavaluzzi John graika Post-modernism Sharon gibbons Elizabeth m. meylor Rex dale Larry johnson Richard peterson Bruce barf Banco popular plaza gebert Norman lindsey hodel Neill gustafson partyka Susan benson ter Bruce resman Tom non officer Pegine sacker Mark seaburg The franklin institute miller Howard sussman gatis David gaber John pel Oregon museum of Mary lenzmeier Dennis George gorbatenko

knecht Robert vestal omnitheater Rosanne Austin farley Gene Joseph mamayek Gene Henry crown space cen ter lasley Erin dunn Shan fitzgerald Mike gott Henry waldenberger Sally enders Rhonda Tom olesak Mark lud pilegaard Mark queri science and industry lanz Dennis bussell Connie johnson Gerald yne mussetter Parvaneh libera Steve skarvan Parc de la villette Michael rekhtman Arthur kelly Richard roggow Susan jacobson Dan rominski Kurt johnson Bob stark Fred dukatz Saint marys hospital Mary lynn anderson Tom johnson Terry penman Ken dowell Mark forsberg Tim gaumond Larry ko Stan simon New melleray abbey David arkin Geoff warner Dan morseth Debbie ahlm Ruth prebil Tony cioper Mary bodene Nancy sonnenberg Luther college Gary johnson David galey Rachel feldberg

CHAPTER VII

ON THE VERGE

Mike Niemeyer

Greenhouse-style conference rooms inside Honeywell's Computer Center allowed employees to monitor equipment while enjoying natural light.

The mid-1970s saw the emergence of a new trend in American architecture — Post-Modernism. Reflecting growing impatience with the "less is more" theories of the early Modernists, leading architects such as Michael Graves, Robert Venturi, and Charles Moore began to use a more decorative style with distinct influences from the past. A greater range of colors came back into vogue, Art Deco reappeared, and classic elements became popular. To top off the movement, Philip Johnson and John Burgee designed the top of the New York AT&T tower, completed in 1982, with a Chippendale curve.

In Minnesota, however, architects were more impressed by Johnson's 1972 IDS building. At Hammel Green and Abrahamson, Post-Modernism was something to be talked about, but only the classic elements used in logical planning or detail were adopted in the company's architecture.

Signaling new opportunity for all architects, business throughout the country began to climb out of the recession about 1974. The firm again hired bright young staff members: architects Kurt Dale, Bill Kokotovich, and Ron Syverson in 1973; engineers Gary Hall and Bob Kaczke and architects Loren Ahles, Bruce Jilk, and Juan Stoleson in 1974. As optimism grew, management saw good years ahead and an expanding practice, vital to the ambitions of many key staff members. Growth was a continuing objective.

Honeywell

The Minneapolis-based Honeywell Corporation faced a major decision about this time — to expand its headquarters in the company's old factory buildings in the city or move to a new complex in the suburbs. Committed to the central city, management chose to stay at its historic headquarters and asked HGA for ideas. The design team proposed several concepts for an urban campus of remodeled and new buildings set amid a landscaped park on the existing 13-acre site. Selecting one of these plans, Honeywell, then under the leadership of its CEO, Edson Spencer, showed its continued faith in the community.

Preceding Page:
Janz/Abrahamson
Arc De Triomphe
conference room.

"We would never have done a Duncan Phyfe pediment."
Curt Green

For Honeywell Plaza, the HGA team (under the leadership of Curt Green, Mike Niemeyer, and Dick Brownlee) developed the Honeywell image — red brick with ribbons of dark tinted glass that blended with the old buildings.

HAMMEL GREEN AND ABRAHAMSON

CHAPTER VII

Jim Goulet

Greg Haley

For the architects, however, there were anxious moments. HGA's fee proposal was termed excessive, so Green sought an opinion from Hammel about a compromise. "Talking things over gave us confidence in dealing with difficult situations," said Green. A lot was at stake since this was the firm's first opportunity to work on an international headquarters for a major corporation. After discussing the problem over lunch, the two returned to Honeywell convinced that the fees they quoted were "right on" and that they could not accept less. The client disagreed and the firm lost the job. One week later, Honeywell called back with a solution, offering work on a wages plus overhead and profit basis. The design teams went back to work and a happy relationship with the client followed.

Converting factories to office headquarters, expanding into a new building, and adding a parking ramp were fast-tracked into Honeywell's highly regulated, competitive contracting procedures. It was a new experience in corporate efficiency for HGA.

The Honeywell Residential Division project won both a *Corporate Report* and MSAIA Honor Award in 1984. A white-gabled canopy announced the main entry; inside, red brick walkways paraded through the building, creating a residential atmosphere.

Honeywell Computer Center

In the next phase of Honeywell headquarters expansion, HGA designed, in 1980, a computer center housing the growing corporate information management group. The red brick materials, glass bands, and architectural forms of the original office were used to unify the complex. The airy, open building featured interior security and light-well conference rooms modeled like greenhouses, allowing employees to enjoy natural lighting while visually monitoring computer equipment beyond the glass walls. According to project manager Greg Haley, "The Honeywell computer room design was innovative, handling one of the largest installations of computers known at that time."

"Aesthetics and engineering are mutually dependent."
Gary Hall

CHAPTER VII

Honeywell Residential Headquarters

The HGA team was called on again in 1982 to consolidate Honeywell's large Residential Division under one roof. After two studies of other sites, Honeywell selected what had been one of its main manufacturing plants in Golden Valley. Corporate offices had been spread out in five different locations, and the designers were challenged to give a strong corporate image to what had been a 1950s solid-walled, concrete warehouse. The old structure presented problems. How could an intermediate mezzanine level be added? HGA engineers did a survey to determine how the building behaved structurally. "We found that it had settled dramatically," said Jim Goulet, an authority on midwestern soil conditions and topography. He explained that the original basement had spread footings and that some of the underlying soils were predominantly organic. The heavier load of an extra floor would necessitate a deeper foundation system penetrating the poor-quality soils. "We had to do low-head caisson drilling, using specially modified equipment to fit the space," said Goulet. In another example of innovation on the part of HGA engineers, the new plan gave the client 60 percent more usable office space.

To relieve large expanses of horizontal space, two-story, gabled skylight roofs lit pedestrian circulation paths divided into six areas of 20,000 square feet each, while a bronze-tinted glass curtain wall brought in even more light.

CHAPTER VII

Pillsbury, Interior Architecture: HGA's Second Joint Venture

A completely different corporate project came to HGA through former partner George Klein, who had opened his own office in 1977. The Gerald Hines Corporation, a large Houston developer, was then building an office tower for First Bank with The Pillsbury Company as the major tenant. Skidmore, Owings & Merrill of Chicago was the architect. While playing tennis with a company space planner, Klein heard that Pillsbury was interviewing firms for interior design.

The next day Klein went into action, calling his HGA friends and contacting the Dayton Company's Contract Division. The three firms formed a joint venture known as the Pillsbury Design Team (PDT) that collectively presented first-rate credentials and, in December 1977, was awarded the contract. Lee Dahlen, HGA's contract specialist, handled the negotiations. Principal Bruce Abrahamson led the HGA design team: Eldon Burow, Julie Snow, Ramy Gill, and engineers Bob Parupsky and Gary Hall. Klein coordinated the effort for the three firms.

The huge interior design project included the upper 25 floors of the 40-story north tower of Pillsbury Center and provided offices for 1,500 employees. Only 10 percent of the offices were private; 90 percent were open. Work stations, executive offices, presentation rooms, and test kitchens were part of the plan. The interiors reflected warmth and dignity. Then, with a stacking diagram for adjacencies of space partially complete, Pillsbury acquired Green Giant in 1979 and the scheme had to be redone.

HGA's engineers played a big role in the Pillsbury project, not only as part of PDT but also by being retained directly to work with Pillsbury's engineering staff in designing food process operations at production facilities elsewhere. "It became evident that we had to be at the cutting edge of high-rise construction because we were dealing with engineering specialists from all over the country," recalled Gary Hall, electrical engineering manager. For Pillsbury Center, HGA engineers designed integrated systems for energy management and security, an on-site computer facility, and computerized audio-visual systems.

General Mills

In 1975, another major corporation, General Mills, selected HGA to add six stories atop the four-story west wing of its corporate headquarters in Golden Valley. When an energy crisis hit the country, the project was delayed for two years, until 1977. From an engineering standpoint, it was a complex job, requiring strict energy management, fire control systems, substation and standby power, acoustics/sound masking, well-water cooling sys-

Pillsbury executive suite stairway. In 1981 The Pillsbury Company, headed by William Spoor, proudly moved into the Center, retaining its historic presence in the heart of the city it helped to build.

"Architecture is a rational art."
HGA anonymous

CHAPTER VII

tems, and a unique central air system. HGA's design team — principal Curt Green, project manager Dick Babcock, designer Ted Butler, mechanical engineers Harry Wilcox and Bob Kaczke, and electrical engineer Gary Hall — worked diligently with the client's engineering group to meet the exacting demands. For the exterior solution, after looking at alternatives, the designers regained the perimeter space between the granite columns and the deeply recessed shaded windows of the original Skidmore, Owings & Merrill design. With new reflective glass that offered heat/gain shielding, the window walls were set flush with the face of the building, giving the client an additional floor of space. Elevators were repositioned in a tower adjacent to one corner of the structure, making for more flexible interior space. During construction, General Mills operations, as well as the Betty Crocker Kitchen tours, went on without interruption.

In 1978, the 10-story building of charcoal granite was completed, proving to the corporate community that HGA could handle work of major proportions and engineering complexity.

Omnitheaters

HGA entered the space age in 1976 when the Science Museum of Minnesota retained the firm to design its new home in downtown St. Paul. A new planetarium was needed, and the entire complex had to be linked with its neighbor across the street, the existing Arts and Science Center. The budget was stringent, yet the facility was to contain the museum's most arresting feature — an omnitheater with a 76-foot domed screen, elevated seating for 350, and new inventions in projection equipment.

Omnimax films had already been attracting throngs to the new space theater of the San Diego Hall of Science. People were

One of the design teams discuss project options

HGA's six-story addition to General Mills Corporate Headquarters in Golden Valley, Minnesota was completed in 1978.

"Bruce thought I was gutsy...
I became one of the guys."
Julie Snow

CHAPTER VII

fascinated with the sensational new medium, made possible by the invention of 70-millimeter film, and fish-eye camera lenses and projection equipment. In Omnimax films (dubbed "the ultimate trip" by a national magazine), audiences found a totally new experience, almost like being projected into outer space. Across the country, science museum directors and boards, who had been seeing a downturn in attendance, suddenly began to perk up.

HGA's design team, led by principal Bruce Abrahamson and project architect Juan Stoleson, shared the excitement of the Science Museum and began working closely with its Board of Directors, Director Phil Taylor, and former director of the San Diego Space Theater, Mike Sullivan, who acted as space theater consultant. St. Paul attorney Jack Hoeschler served as project coordinator for the museum. "You could always tell the architects by their corduroy jackets and bow ties. Abrahamson, a very creative guy, was always the consummate partner in charge. The first design had us all elated, but the contractors called it too expensive, so it was back to the drawing board," said Hoeschler. The exterior design was modified, retaining a curving facade, with bright red canopy boldly marking the main entrance.

"The most critical design aspect centered around the circular William L. McKnight 3M Omnitheater," said Stoleson. Engineer Glenn Hawkinson had to design mechanical systems in harmony with the sensitive and powerful audiovisual systems. "Those speakers can rattle ductwork or anything else that's not nailed down."

The new building rose in three open levels, containing a variety of scientific exhibitions, flying bridges, and the most technically advanced movie theater in the world. In the circular theater the image surrounded the audience, creating a three-dimensional experience.

For the architects, the experience meant a whole new set of expertise that led to HGA's establishment as the leading architectural firm in the highly specialized field of space theaters. Commissions have included:

- The Alabama Space and Rocket Center, Huntsville (1982)
- Fort Worth Museum of Science and History (1982)
- Boston's Museum of Science, Mugar Omnitheater (1987)
- Pittsburgh Science Center, Omnimax Theater (estimated opening 1990)

Since opening in 1978, the McKnight Omnitheater has spurred renewed interest in the museum's programs and membership.

CHAPTER VII

Entrance to the Omnimax theater

- Banco Popular Plaza Omnitheater, San Juan, Puerto Rico (As working drawings were completed in 1987, the bank dropped the project.)
- Henry Crown Space Center, Museum of Science and Industry, Chicago (1986)
- The Franklin Institute, Omnimax Theater, Philadelphia (estimated opening 1990)
- Oregon Museum of Science and Industry, Portland (estimated opening 1990)

In addition, HGA obtained its first international commission in December 1980 from a museum in Paris, the Parc de la Villette, to do a feasibility study for a projected space theater addition. In 1981, however, when a new premier assumed power in that country, the American architects were dismissed in favor of a French firm. Since then, museums in Stockholm, The Hague, Sydney, Ottawa, and Great Britain have sought the firm's expertise.

For project architect Stoleson, one thrilling occasion was the July 1986 opening of the Henry Crown Space Center for the Museum of Science and Industry in Chicago. "Even NBC's *Today Show* broadcast live from the center that day. There were all kinds of celebrities: five astronauts and the biggest gathering of VIPs I had ever seen, including the director of NASA, Jim Beggs," said Stoleson. The Omnimax film premiered that evening was *The Dream Is Alive*, documenting America's space program.

This project for the Chicago museum, its first addition since 1893, was a particular challenge to HGA architects and engineers because they had to house a new Omnimax theater in a domed structure while relating the new building to the old in design and materials. To do this, they used a limestone base, a light metal roof cap, copper cladding, and clay tiles similar to the

Opening directly to the street from a soaring glass-enclosed lobby, the new Science Museum of Minnesota has contributed substantially to downtown St. Paul's revitalization.

Juan Stoleson

Three-dimensional reality on a two-dimensional screen

Exhibition space for the museum's collections

"We've made Omnitheaters a theatrical experience by displaying the projection equipment."
Bruce Abrahamson

HAMMEL GREEN AND ABRAHAMSON

The Henry Crown Space Center reflected the classical symmetry of the original Museum of Science and Industry while functioning as a contemporary tourist attraction. First-year attendance surpassed all projections.

CHAPTER VII

original museum's central rotunda. Siting the building next to a reflecting pond, they attached the domed theater to the old building with a glass-enclosed link housing displays, a new restaurant, and a gift shop. The dome-shaped structure created acoustical problems also requiring special solutions, according to Yanak Shagalov, senior project structural engineer in HGA's newly formed structural engineering department.

Saint Marys Hospital, Rochester

In the mid-1970s, with George Riches heading HGA's team of health care specialists, the firm entered into a long relationship with Saint Marys Hospital of Rochester, Minnesota.

Saint Marys, a famous health care institution offering patients the latest in health care technology, derived its character from the presence of the Franciscan Sisters who started the hospital in 1889. It was Rochester's first hospital and has continued to grow under the nuns' persevering administration.

By 1975, Saint Marys had four main buildings linked in a quadrangle. Still, it was becoming crowded and badly in need of more surgical space and other modern facilities. In an architectural search, Naramore Bain Brady Johnson (NBBJ) of Seattle was selected for its expertise in surgery suite planning and HGA as local architect, on its reputation for quality service. The two firms formed a joint venture, with Jim Jonassen the NBBJ principal, Riches the HGA principal, and Jerry Olson project manager. Working closely, the team designed an eight-story addition, expanding the hospital by one-third.

At the heart of the project was a new surgical suite, containing 36 major and eight minor operating rooms (the size of two football fields). The operating rooms were grouped around

Attending the opening of the Henry Crown Space Center in 1986 were HGA team leaders Gary Reetz (left) and Juan Stoleson (right) with consultant Michael Sullivan and Chicago associate architect Eugene Cook.

> "I often tell new clients that they're going to be very involved in a project with us. We spend a lot of time and energy that way."
> George Riches

CHAPTER VII

central sterile supply areas like a racetrack. The new space contained patient floors, expanded cafeteria facilities, rehabilitation, physical medicine, intensive care, radiology, admissions, emergency, support services, and a sunny new lobby with taxi entrance.

"Sister Generose, the hospital administrator, was really the driving force behind the surgical expansion," said Riches. "We would bring down hundreds and hundreds of drawings. She would pore over these, studying them 16 hours a day, and then ask incredibly detailed questions such as, 'Why is that handrail an eight-inch piece of oak?'"

In tribute to the hospital's third administrator, the new red brick structure was named the Mary Brigh Building, for Sister Mary Brigh Cassidy, at dedication ceremonies in 1980. As an amenity for patients and in keeping with the Saint Marys philosophy of maintaining green space with flowers and outdoor sculpture as a serene space for visitors and patients, a landscaped courtyard was designed by Kurt Rogness and Dean Abbott. Since 1982 HGA has handled many other Saint Marys projects involving remodeling, master planning, and other continuing work.

HGA's Jerry Olson continued as a principal member of the health care team servicing Saint Marys and Mayo later. Eventually he became director of the firm's technical architecture division. Well known for his technical abilities, Olson said he derives a great deal of personal satisfaction from his work on complex medical facilities.

New Melleray Abbey

By 1976 Ted Butler, who had already made his mark as a talented architectural designer, was working with nationally known liturgical design consultant Frank Kacmarcik on various religious facilities across the country. They were selected by the Trappist monks in a 110-year-old monastery in Dubuque, Iowa, to do a complete interior renovation of their old stone and wood building.

What the designers set out to accomplish was not a restoration per se, but an adaptive re-use. The old quadrangle wing, with chapel, offices, and dining space, was gutted to create the abbey church. At the time work began, plaster was falling off some walls, and stone had begun to deteriorate along the foundations. Following the designer's concept, the monks stripped away the plaster to the original stone and removed unnecessary ornamentation, interior walls and partitions, plus the second floor of the original building. The plan succeeded. The new church had unique proportions — 225 feet long, 28 feet wide, and 40 feet high — resulting in a space of uplifting serenity.

Sister Generose reviewed every detail of the Saint Marys expansion.

"When a snowstorm stranded us in Dubuque, Iowa, Father Joseph offered to drive us to the Waterloo airport. He hadn't talked to anyone for 20 years because of the oath of silence, but it had been recently removed. No wonder he talked steady for 2½ hours without stopping!"
Ted Butler

HAMMEL GREEN AND ABRAHAMSON

CHAPTER VII

This beautifully simple renovation of the New Melleray Abbey won a 1976 MSAIA award and a 1977 national AIA award. The jury commented: "This remodeling of a two-story wing of a Cistercian monastery has resulted in a handsome abbey church. The good sense of retaining the exterior intact, combined with the courageous decision to expose the masonry wall and timber trusses, has created a sanctuary of great proportions, simplicity and serenity."

HAMMEL GREEN AND ABRAHAMSON

CHAPTER VII

Luther College, Jensen Hall of Music

Of all towns in the United States, Decorah, Iowa, probably has the strongest ties to Norway, through Luther College and the Vesterheim Museum. The college needed to consolidate its music department, which in the late 1970s was scattered around the campus. HGA's design team, headed by principal Curt Green with designer John Justus and project architects Vlad Chahovskoy and Ramy Gill, created a two-story brick building recalling the form and materials of adjacent buildings. The designers used sloped red tile roofs, red brick, and limestone banding.

A striking feature of the interior was a "student street" bisecting the building. Carpet-tiled floors, arched lamps, and gabled entry vestibules symbolized the houses along a street in Bergen, Norway. Flanking the street were the rehearsal and recital rooms, practice rooms, studios, classrooms, and faculty offices, all marked with gabled entrances. Jensen Hall was also made energy efficient with skylights flooding the "street" and permitting passive solar gain in winter and delighting students and faculty.

The Luther College Music Hall brought in another MSAIA Honor Award in 1983.

Colonial Church of Edina

When Dick Hammel and Ted Butler began studies for the Colonial Church of Edina in 1971, little did they know what they started. Membership had risen dramatically to 2,270, only eight years after the Reverend Arthur A. Rouner, Jr. had been selected to head the ministry. As programs continued to expand, the democratic-minded church held many meetings with the architects before it made the decision to move. In 1974, the congregation voted to buy a 23-acre site just half a mile away. It still wanted a "puritan" building, but one with a variety of multi-purpose spaces suited to its social and community outreach programs.

"What is colonial architecture?"

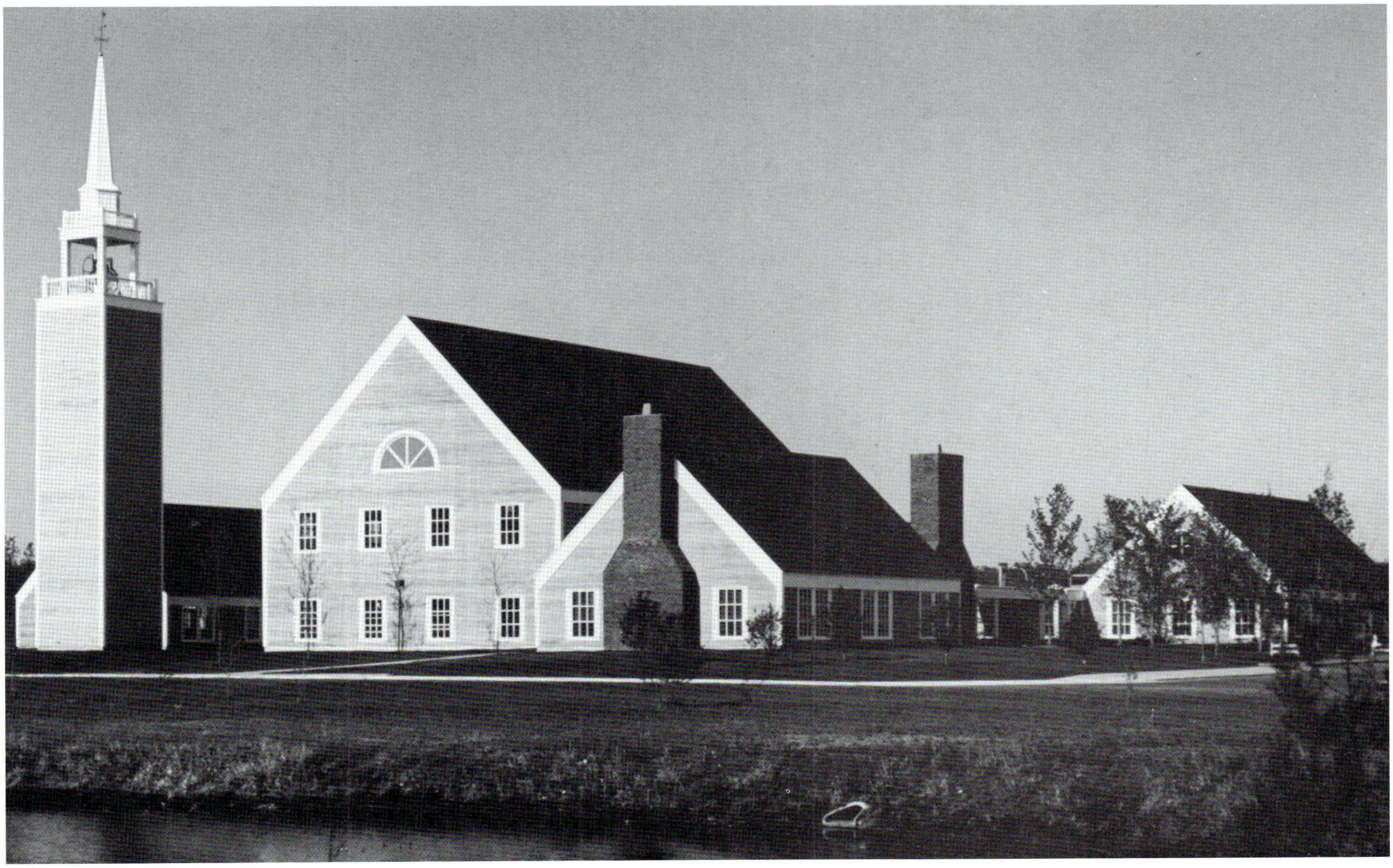

Design

Creating for God's Glory

Church architects are turning out striking new buildings

During most of the post–World War II era, offices, apartments and even billboards have dwarfed church steeples. In response, religious buildings have frantically vied for attention with bizarre bell towers, frenzied A-frames and strange paraboloids. But until recently, few churches have managed to convey a religious quality beyond that of a contorted steeple or a neon JESUS SAVES sign.

All that seems to be undergoing considerable change. Many church architects are now producing more exciting work than colleagues who are straining to overcome the discredited, bare and square look of modern office towers and apartment houses. "If you had to pick a single piece of decent architecture that could rightfully be called post-modern," says William Houseman, editor of *Architecture Minnesota*, "the Colonial Church of Edina, Minn., might well be it."

The Colonial Church, on the outskirts of Minneapolis, was designed by Architect Richard F. Hammel, 58, of Hammel Green Abrahamson, Inc., a Minneapolis-based firm. "Designing religious buildings is arduous," says Hammel. "It took six years of discussions and hard work with the congregation and its pastor, Dr. Arthur Rouner Jr., to achieve a harmonious understanding of the function and meaning of their church. But it is wonderful work, because something other than dollars is valued. You are designing for the celebration of human life."

The church, which opened in 1978, is a kind of minivillage on a 22-acre site along a man-made lake. It consists of a meetinghouse or sanctuary that seats 1,000, a freestanding tower, a parlor for small weddings and other assemblies, a social hall, a youth center and a library with staff offices. It was conceived in the Pilgrim and Puritan tradition of early New England churches, but its form is traditional only in that the white-trimmed gray clapboard and spire convey a sense of historic continuity. The architecture is closer to the modern simplicity of Mies van der Rohe than the baroque intricacy of Sir Christopher Wren.

Another enchanting example of contemporary architecture is also religious—the 22-month-old Thorncrown Chapel in Eureka Springs, Ark. It is one of the most popular and widely publicized of new American buildings. The secluded chapel, which seats about 130, won an award for excellence from the American Institute of Architects and was sought out last year by 120,000 visitors. Noting its striking qualities, the A.I.A. *Journal* says, "It is a building of great integrity."

At once familiar and novel, the chapel was built for wayfarers rather than a resident congregation. No larger than a tall barn, it stands at the bend of a wooded trail, high in the Ozark Mountains. An almost transparent structure of mostly timber and glass, it seems to be one with the surrounding woods and rocks. The chapel's architect, E. Fay Jones of Fayetteville, Ark., who studied with Frank Lloyd Wright, describes it as a kind of reversed of gothic cathedral architecture. The trusses inside the structure form a repetitive, rhythmic lattice pattern as evocative as a Bach fugue.

Among the most active churches in the U.S. is the small and simple St. Peter's Lutheran Church on Lexington Avenue in midtown Manhattan. St. Peter's, which opened in 1977, adorns the base of Hugh Stubbins Jr.'s 59-story Citicorp Center. Although it is not, strictly speaking, part of the Citicorp skyscraper, it too was designed by Stubbins and fits masterfully into his overall architectural vision. Stubbins' church holds its own at the foot of the somewhat brutish 915-ft. Citicorp tower. The church's uncluttered, skylit interiors were created by Vignelli Associates using natural colors and materials. Sculptor Louise Nevelson designed the church's small but exquisite Erol Beker Chapel of the Good Shepherd. St. Peter's is indeed a sanctuary in a cold and hectic city.

All three of these churches are pointing the way toward a vital new

The timber-and-glass Thorncrown Chapel: a wayfarer's haven

A sanctuary, right, adorns Colonial Church minivillage, below

At the foot of Citicorp Center, worshipers gather at St. Peter's

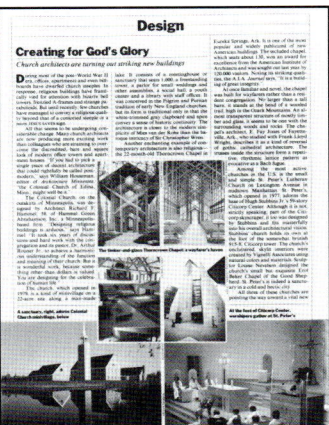

In 1980, the AIA selected Colonial Church of Edina for national honors, calling it "a subtle, integrated building group that responds to the users' needs."

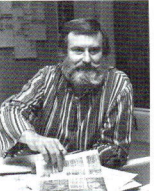

Ted Butler

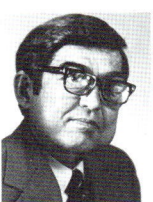

Dick Hammel

Classic windows and forms are examples of post-modern architecture at Colonial Church.

In an interview with *Time* (April 1982) Dick Hammel said: **It took six years of discussions and hard work with the congregation and its pastor Dr. Arthur Rouner, Jr., to achieve a harmonious understanding of the function and meaning of their church. But it is wonderful work because something other than dollars is valued. You are designing for the celebration of human life.**

CHAPTER VII

For principal architect Hammel, the Reverend Rouner, and the building committee chaired by Charles Geer, it was the beginning of a debate about colonial architecture. Hammel and Rouner traveled to Barnstable, Massachusetts, where the minister, a native New Englander, knew of a small church dating to the arrival of the Pilgrims. Hammel, impressed by its simplicity, came back determined to create a church making a contemporary statement of Colonial's puritan religious and architectural history.

In the winter of 1979, the new Colonial Church of Edina opened to wide acclaim. Members were absolutely delighted with the gray clapboard, white-trimmed, mini-New England village style. The once swampy land now looked like a park, with five gabled-roof components around an open courtyard. HGA civil engineer Jim Goulet said, "This was one of the first buildings that we literally built in the middle of a marsh." Since the area was a backwater to Nine-Mile Creek and also a sedimentation basin for storm water, HGA engineers had to transform the entire site, even creating a small island facing the highway.

The bell tower, 125 feet tall, stood alone, a symbol of a religious community. "When we designed the church, we were doing it in simple Post-Modern form. We used the bell tower as a sculptural element composed in the framework of all the buildings," said Butler. To reduce the scale of such a large complex, the designers developed a village of buildings housing a sanctuary or "meeting house," seminar rooms, lounges, and a great hall (fellowship lounge), linking them with a main street walkway. The result was a complete New England-style village. For the interior, the design team chose a warm palette of honey-colored woods and other basic materials — exposed posts, beams, and trusses, as seen in early colonial barns.

Proposed Design Projects

For all architects, even the most ingenious designs do not always become bricks and mortar. Here are a few projects that HGA designers nevertheless considered achievements.

Control Data Executive Office, Bloomington, Minnesota

Described as a "contemplative building for a steeply sloping site," the Control Data Executive Office was tackled by principal Curt Green and designer Ted Butler. They proposed a four-level building that stepped down the slope towards the Minnesota River. Later, the company determined it needed a much larger facility and called HGA for a proposal. The schedule was so abbreviated that the young firm included overtime wages in its proposed fee. Result? They lost the opportunity for years of work with Control Data.

The Bloomington Civic Center

In 1966 HGA was commissioned to study a projected civic center site, on 90 acres of public land adjacent to the projected site for Normandale Junior College. The architects proposed a master civic center plan, and a community ice center was the first building constructed. Four years later the city asked the firm to update the plan to include a municipal office building. Designers Bruce Abrahamson and Jim Wengler presented a detailed plan illustrating how a new civic center complete with tower, multi-story buildings, parking ramps, youth center, auditorium and public plaza could become the dynamic new heart of Bloomington. But the project would have required major expenditures that the city was not ready to take on, and it was finally abandoned.

Hammel was struck by the simplicity of the West Barnstable Church in Cape Cod saying

"It's an inspiring model of modern architecture because of the exposed beams and pine benches."

CHAPTER VII

The Executive Office Building for Control Data Corporation won a citation from *Progressive Architecture* in January 1970.

Model of HGA's winning design for the Iranian National Library. Competition results narrowed to approximately ten winners, with HGA's submission one of only two finalists from the United States.

The Pahlavi National Library, Tehran, Iran

The government of Iran sponsored a worldwide design competition in 1977 for a monumental national Iranian library to be located on a large public square in the heart of the government center of Tehran. The huge structure was to include a research library, a public library, and an Iranian studies center.

HGA had an Iranian connection. Ali Vahajji, a former mechanical engineer for the firm who had returned to Tehran, called Bruce Abrahamson and suggested a collaborative effort. Abrahamson flew to Tehran, making a crash effort to understand Islamic culture and architecture. On his return, Abrahamson assembled a design team of young architects including Dan Avchen, Loren Ahles, Martha Yunker, and Bob Lundgren. Working in "design charettes," they devised an elaborate, strikingly dramatic structure relating to Near Eastern classical forms. The building was intended to become a monument to Pahlavi, the Shah of Iran, but with his deposition, the library was never built.

Minneapolis Domed Stadium

In 1975 Minneapolis movers and shakers became determined that the city should erect a covered stadium downtown to keep the Minnesota Vikings and Minnesota Twins in the state and to help build tourism for the cities. The issue grew into a heated controversy involving the Minneapolis Chamber of Commerce, the City of Minneapolis, and the Minnesota Legislature. The prospect excited many architects around the country, including HGA.

"Because we wanted to become more active on the urban scene and strongly believed that the stadium should be in Minneapolis, we got into the act," said Curt Green. With a sixth sense for politics, Hammel contacted former mayor Art Naftalin. Mean-

> "Some of our best designs are in the drawer."
> Curt Green

CHAPTER VII

while, Seattle architects (NBBJ) for the King County Dome Stadium called on Abrahamson in search of a local architect to associate with in the competition for the domed stadium. Soon after, the three HGA principals and Naftalin flew to Seattle to see for themselves a concrete dome under construction there.

After the visit, they began meeting informally with several leaders of the Minneapolis Chamber of Commerce — Bower Hawthorne, Charles Krusell, Harvey MacKay, and Bill McGrann — to identify a site and discuss a general design. A plan emerged with Naftalin urging HGA to come up with a concept for the Seven Corners site and to host a luncheon at which they would present their drawings to the chamber's group of stadium promoters. Hammel immediately began organizing the event while Abrahamson and Green marshalled a design team including NBBJ. "Almost overnight HGA whomped up renderings of a full-scale domed stadium concept, which could serve the U of M too," recalled Naftalin. HGA's drawings, done "on spec" were formally presented in spring of 1976 at a luncheon, by then grown to a public event for about 90 state and local leaders.

The stadium issue was being studied informally by the Legislature, and competition had intensified for sites. In 1977, the Legislature created the Metropolitan Sports Facilities Commission, to decide what kind of stadium should be built and where. In the midst of the site competition, a group for the City of Minneapolis had championed a stadium on the Industry Square site because it was an urban renewal area where the city already owned land. It was also close to the U of M. The chamber hired HGA to do a study for a multi-use stadium at that site. It had full endorsement of the city and was presented to the Legislature as such.

After many meetings, appearances at the Legislature,

The HGA scheme for a domed stadium suitable for professional football, baseball, international soccer, and U of M football made it into all the newspapers and TV newscasts.

CHAPTER VII

intense planning sessions, and heated debate, the city's site as presented in the HGA proposal was selected. Then the sky fell in! The stadium commission voted to send the architectural commission out of town. Although it did not get the job, HGA had made a contribution to the city and enhanced its own reputation.

Enlarging Ownership

In a major commitment to growth, HGA's three founding principals decided to open up ownership of the firm in 1978 by bringing in additional stockholders. There had been only seven stockholders previously — Hammel, Green, and Abrahamson, plus Dahlen, Sorensen, Babcock, and Butler. (Engineers Bob Gish, Dave Martin, and Ken Schultz and architects George Klein, Jr. and Hugh Peacock had been stockholders before leaving the firm.)

HGA had now reached its 25th year, a time for reassessment and future projection. "The three founders knew they had to think seriously about bringing in the next generation," said secretary-treasurer Lee Dahlen. In principle, the board agreed that to perpetuate the firm, it was essential to enlarge the ownership. It was a move designed to give others not only an increased sense of belonging, but also a new awareness of responsibility to themselves and to the firm, according to Dahlen. "By advancing key people to the principal level, we felt they would become more active in the marketplace and they would have the tools to help move the firm ahead," said Bruce Abrahamson.

Accordingly, the board offered equal shares of stock to 13 others: architects Bill Anderson, Duane Blanchard, Perry Bolin, Eldon Burow, Jerry Olson, George Riches, and Kurt Rogness; engineers Jim Goulet, Gary Hall, Dennis Leslie, Bob Parupsky, and Harry Wilcox; and Rod Erickson of specifications. Bringing engi-

Topped with an air-supported Teflon-coated fiberglass roof, the stadium provided seating for more than 65,000.

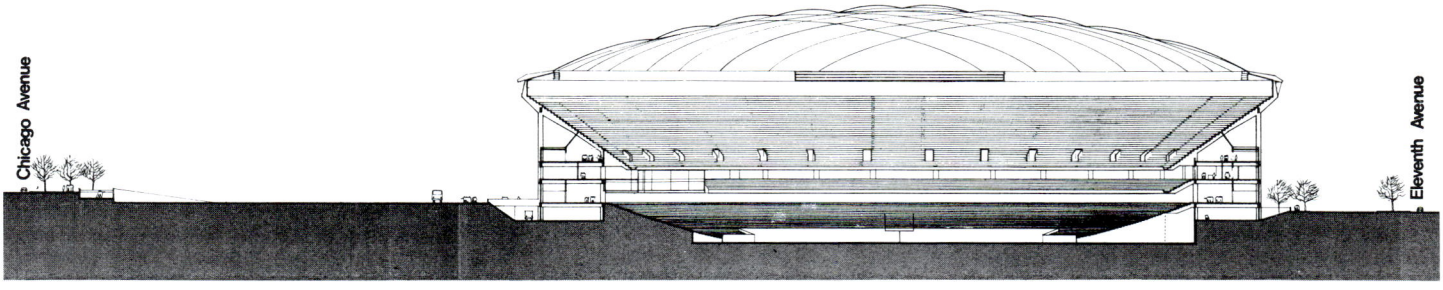

In 1989, HGA conducted a feasibility analysis for a retractable roof for the Hubert H. Humphrey Metrodome. While doing research, chief engineer Harry Wilcox learned that the Roman Coliseum had a removable cover for use in inclement weather.
"If the Romans did it, so can we!"
Harry Wilcox

Congratulations on Super Bowl '92!

CHAPTER VII

neers back into ownership positions confirmed the firm's stance as an architecture/engineering organization. All new stockholders ranging in age from 35 to 45 years, represented the second generation.

The newly expanded ownership team was well received, and the firm continued to grow. In the next two years, however, agitation grew among members of the second generation who wanted a more defined ownership transfer plan that addressed retirement, death, and resignation. Some painful confrontations and long discussions ensued in the summer of 1980. Curt Green, as president, initiated a weekend officers' retreat with a professional industry moderator. The purpose of the retreat was to thrash out disagreements and arrive at a consensus.

As a result, a transfer-of-ownership plan began to unfold. Hammel, Green, and Abrahamson met with their attorneys at Briggs and Morgan to make the plan official. Still, the situation remained delicate. In 1982, George Riches, Ted Butler, and Kurt Rogness were offered major blocks of stock. That year a professional management consultant, Enion Associates, was brought in for a management and organization study. Recommendations followed and the next year a restructuring of operations took place with emphasis on strong project management. "Everyone became more accountable," said director of engineering Harry Wilcox. "We had finally arrived at the large firm concept, so we had to reorganize ourselves to deal with future growth." HGA began to change from a studio system to a departmental organization.

The reorganization process did not change HGA's basic team approach to architecture, but the staff became more specialized, with stronger project managers working under the guidance of principal architects and engineers.

The Stockholders in 1980.

In a discussion of HGA's mission, Dick Hammel's response was short and crisp,
"To stay in business."

CHAPTER - VIII

Lisa schaefer Mark bengtson Steve miller Dave jones Rawley brodeen Rodger lambert Annette hardy David fey Sharon roe Joan stauffer Ellen hatfield Linda morrissey Pongskorn jew Control data Ron hernandez Mary mcmenamy Peter curtis David howd Kris pouti Vince james Don wong Tom vermeland City of bloomington Marth brewster Gretchen eckhardt Shirajoy abry Yvonne christensen John olfelt Laurel parriott Jon gravender John knowland Pahlavi national library Roger santelman Scot anderson Mike ossian Judy lewis Shari Group health Gary hul ball olson Tom whit Eino mehta Paul ander neapolis children's fan Mark brennan Mark ugowski Rick fer Bart baker Tom hospital Terry jones rice montiel Craig ald emy Rebecca greco Chris dillon Saint jos

Diane blair Jeff zieba gould Duke beeson ton Donna esch Kim comb Harry cizewski son Kelli gaborsky Min medical center Tim ste Carolyn hartmann hintz Laurie kruhoef johnson Saint john's Michell cassioppi Pat rich Elizabeth barthel Murray schomburg eph's hospital David ber cher Jeff zutz Katherin kiefer Amit dhar Stephen fiskum Steve pawliszko Stephen gentilini Mark hoel The palmer group Bob rothman Eric krempa Jim butler Ella kogan Peter cavaluzzi Joanne dircz Penny saiki John bauch Saint john's university Duane thorpe Matt gilbertson Juanita bos Bart nelson Patty miller Debbie edwards Daniel houlihan Stan sivertsen Church of saint peter Al wenzel Don haataja Tom anderson Mark heller Greg harrom Zina dovskin Henry grabowski Charlotte axt Chapel of seven dolors David gotham Louise fontaine Tony staeger Larry ko Sheryl brolander Peggy hepp

CHAPTER VIII

THE 1980S EXPANSION

Dan Avchen

Tom Swearingen

Post-Modernism was in full swing at the start of the 1980s. It had become the fashion, particularly on both coasts. At the same time, however, a ground swell of opposition was developing, with some architects calling the trend a passing style. Midwestern reaction, in fact, was typically restrained. "Post-Modernism gave us a whole new palette for design that we'd never thought of before — in materials and construction, the use of more decorative elements...a more humanistic approach," said Curt Green. This was reflected at HGA, where the architects felt freer to experiment with form, livelier design, and more engaging spaces. They found that the use of more ornamentation was not only acceptable, but preferred by clients.

The Move to Downtown Minneapolis

Having made a major commitment to growth, HGA was running out of office space for its staff, still located primarily in the Hubbard Building in St. Paul, with additional space leased in the Park Plaza Building in Minneapolis. Management began a serious search for new space in downtown Minneapolis which it considered the state's vital center for business.

The search included an old hydro-power plant near the Falls of St. Anthony, some river warehouses, the Thresher Building and others. Finally, HGA located a 1920s automobile showroom (the old Boyer Ford building at 12th Street and Harmon Place in downtown Minneapolis), and a developer from whom they could lease the building. It was a sturdy 60 year old three-story brick structure that offered good possibilities for remodeling. Winning an in-house design competition, Dan Avchen (who became a stockholder and principal in 1981) amplified the open-office concept, linking the floors with a cascading skylit stairway. The old interior wooden beams and brick walls were retained and new windows installed throughout. In September 1981, a delighted staff of approximately 150 architects, engineers, planners, and designers moved into the firm's new home at 1201 Harmon Place. It was a stimulating environment that marked a turning point in HGA's evolution as a full-service architectural/engineering office.

A significant renovation of the 1914 chapel at the College of Saint Benedict was completed in 1982 with Ted Butler as principal.

MSAIA nominated HGA for the AIA's national firm-of-the-year award, the first such nomination for a Minnesota-based firm.

The new office at 1201 was a modest place out of the high rent district, and with parking. A potential client touring the building said, **"We should hire these people so they could afford ceilings in their office."**

CHAPTER VIII

Staff Expansion and Departmentalizing

The move brought further organization of the various disciplines to HGA, which maintained its team approach. This new structuring of specialist groups provided an experienced response to an array of diverse clients. Each project continued under the direction of a principal architect or engineer. "This is a personal service business," Hammel said.

Project growth brought the need for further staff expansion. In the early 1980s, several eventual stockholders joined the firm: Tom Swearingen and Paul Williams in 1980, Robert Fontaine in 1982, Dennis Lanz in 1983, and Roger Santelman in 1984. Other bright new additions of the 1980s were architects Steve Fiskum, Tom Johnson, Gary Nyberg, Mike Ossian, Gary Reetz, Ted Rozeboom, and Dennis Wallace as well as engineers Dave Galey, Jim Moravek, Gene Partyka, Dick Peterson, Yanak Shagalov, and Al Wenzel. Many of them became stockholders. During the same period, four stockholders resigned: Bill Anderson in 1982, Dick Babcock and Wes Sorenson in 1983, and Eldon Burow in 1985.

In July 1983, management agreed to split the stock one hundred to one, thus creating greater flexibility in the future sale of stock. In 1984, George Riches, who was already refining the restructuring process, was elected president of the company.

HGA's third decade brought new honors to the firm's founders. Bruce Abrahamson was invested as a Fellow of the American Institute of Architects (FAIA) at the national convention in Dallas in 1971, Richard Hammel received the FAIA honor in San Francisco in 1973, and Curt Green became a FAIA recipient in Minneapolis, 1981.

A New Department — Interior Design

Since the firm's inception, its design teams had always planned interior spaces for their clients as part of the total architectural service. "We were trained in the philosophy that the architect did everything," said Bruce Abrahamson. "For the early schools, we didn't get to do too much except choose colors. But where we had the opportunity, we picked out furnishings and

Corporate Report gave the new HGA office one of its Best Office Awards in 1983.

> "People are at their creative best at play; we need to have fun in what we do."
> **HGA Anonymous**

HAMMEL GREEN AND ABRAHAMSON

CHAPTER VIII

Nancy Cameron, Louise Fontaine and Nancy Stark discussing design concepts.

carpets." As the firm's institutional work grew, clients came to realize the need for integrating professional interior design with architectural design. Gradually, the project designer took charge of it all, including the selection of fabrics and furnishings, carpets and lighting, and especially the color palette.

While the staff was still in the Hubbard Building, Ken LeDoux, an architect with a special sense for interiors, became HGA's first architect focusing on interiors (late 1970s) and continued in this discipline until his resignation. His design of the elegant 510 Restaurant dining room was of particular note.

Soon after the move to downtown Minneapolis, HGA hired Robert Fontaine, a multi-talented designer who became the first director of the interior design department, which he saw as an expanded marketing force for the firm. Working seven days a week, he was designer, illustrator, and conceptualizer as the department grew to include 14 staff members. "I believe architects and interior designers have to be linked...architects who practice in this field should be lovers of the true arts," said Fontaine, who brought with him continuing interior work for the Mayo Clinic. This evolved into several health care projects for the interiors department including those for: Group Health, Minneapolis Children's Medical Center, St. John's Hospital, and St. Joseph's Hospital.

With the addition of Eldon Burow as principal and project manager, HGA's interiors department branched out, taking on more corporate work while maintaining educational and health care facilities as part of its services.

In 1982, Fontaine and Burow tackled a significant interiors project for The Palmer Group developers — to renovate a central atrium in a 1914 building for First Trust Center in downtown St. Paul. Originally, railroad magnate James J. Hill owned two buildings on the same block for the Great Northern and Northern Pacific railroads. Each had its own entrance and elevator. "The only way you could get from one building to the other was by going through the presidents' offices," recalled Burow. Between the buildings was a huge atrium which J. J. Hill had initially intended as the lobby of the First National Bank of St. Paul. It had gone through several remodelings, and was "quite ugly", according to Burow.

The developers asked the designers to give life to the central atrium and remake it into viable commercial space with connections to Galtier Plaza and existing skyways. The renovation process revealed long-concealed balconies with handsome wrought-iron railings, beautiful columns, and the original skylights. A central escalator was installed, and other contemporary elements such as lighting were carefully chosen to blend in with the old.

"Paint it black and it'll go away."
Nancy Cameron

"We need more men in this department."
Nancy Stark

CHAPTER VIII

The Mayo Great Hall at the Mayo Clinic Student Center in Rochester won a 1986 ASID honor award for distinguished renovation of a traditional and elegant room providing contemporary space for students to study in comfort.

Gleaming with terrazzo floors, the finished atrium of the First Trust Center was a handsome example of enhancing classic craftsmanship with contemporary design.

CHAPTER VIII

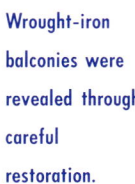

Wrought-iron balconies were revealed through careful restoration.

For First Trust, the renovation completed in 1987 was a resounding success. Later, Burow left HGA to join The Palmer Group, and HGA architect Ronn Carlson became department manager. In 1985, Louise Fontaine, a well-known local interior designer, joined the staff, contributing her talents to such projects as the Radisson Centerplace Hotel, the new law offices for Briggs and Morgan, and the Mayo Medical Center.

In 1988, architect and stockholder Nancy Stark was named director of the interiors department. The same year, Nancy Cameron, interior architect and specialist in lease-hold space planning, joined the department as marketing principal. Cameron, who excelled in programming (planning interior spaces for the specific users' needs) said, "I love this aspect of my work because it's a people process. Designing an environment for the people who work in it enhances the individual. It's the workers' greenhouse that allows them to flourish."

Historic Preservation

The restoration of interior spaces has not been the only historic preservation work of HGA. Architects and engineers have restored a variety of historic structures, renovated worthwhile old buildings with updated mechanical systems, and remodeled antiquated facilities. In 1980, an HGA design team completed the final restoration of St. John's University quadrangle buildings at Collegeville, Minnesota. In keeping with the traditions of this Benedictine university, the interior was returned to its original simplicity by exposing the rich red brick walls and using natural wood framing. The religious design team in particular has excelled in historic renovation projects such as the award-winning Church of St. Peter in Saratoga Springs, New York; New Melleray

The new department also expanded the interiors samples library. In the summer of 1985, the library tripled, becoming a complete Interiors Resource Library, planned for easy access to all materials. A full-time resource librarian, Roxanne Lange, with a contract furnishings background, was hired to assist designers in their search for materials.

"The three colors of modernism were black, white, and grey. "Now we're seeing a yellow base trend for the '90s with colors shifting to yellows, olives and browns, shades we haven't used for years."
Louise Fontaine

HAMMEL GREEN AND ABRAHAMSON

Working with consultant Frank Kacmarcik, the HGA design team preserved the Gothic character and improved the function of the Church of St. Peter in Saratoga Springs, New York originally built in the 1850s.

CHAPTER VIII

Abbey in Dubuque, Iowa; St. Benedict's Chapel in St. Joseph, Minnesota; Chapel of Seven Dolors in Nerinx, Kentucky; St. Mary's Cathedral in St. Cloud, Minnesota; and St. Mary of the Lake Church in White Bear Lake, Minnesota.

The Saint Paul Hotel

The next renovation project turned out to be a hotel, the *grande dame* of the city, the 1910-vintage Saint Paul Hotel. The most popular gathering place in St. Paul for many years, it had fallen into complete disrepair by 1980, and plans for rescue had begun. The developers (Lincoln Hotels of Dallas and the Jefferson Companies of Minneapolis, aided by industrial revenue bonds issued by the St. Paul Port Authority) called on HGA to transform the landmark building into an elegant luxury-class hotel.

When designer Dan Avchen and project manager Gary Reetz first entered the once-proud hotel, "It was entirely occupied by pigeons, and everything was covered with ice," recalled Reetz. Although the exterior could be cleaned and repaired, the interior needed total demolition and redesign. From the start Avchen felt the atmosphere of the building should be preserved: "Originally, it was built in the fine European tradition; we tried to bring that back. It's old, elegant with quiet refinement. We wanted the building to say that."

For the interior, the architects felt it advisable to hire a professional hotel interior designer since this was HGA's first major hotel project. One name stood out — Sarah Tomerlin Lee of Tom Lee, Ltd., Interiors, New York, a delightful grande dame famous for her design of many distinguished old hotels. Working closely with Lee, the design team created a resplendent but intimate lobby, complete with the hotel's three original crystal

The main entrance of the renovated Saint Paul Hotel was wisely relocated to face Rice Park, the new cultural heart of the city.

CHAPTER VIII

chandeliers, a richly appointed bar overlooking the park, and two new ground-floor restaurants. The casino ballroom was retained in its original location. In 1982, after the renovation was complete, Sarah Lee remarked, "Never in my career have I been involved with a building and a city that together evoke so many good feelings in people." In 1989, Avchen and Lee teamed up again to plan a new restaurant for the Saint Paul Hotel's main floor.

Other Hotels

In 1983 Maddux Properties commissioned the firm to design the Radisson University Hotel on a campus site adjacent to Memorial Stadium. Completed in 1985, the dark red brick building blended in well with the U of M's campus architecture.

In 1982 Carlson Companies hired HGA to design its "crown jewel" hotel in the heart of Minneapolis on the site of the popular old Radisson. The building was to include condominiums, offices, and retail space. Economic projections and cost estimates, however, kept this design from proceeding, so the client created a partnership with developer Bechtel of San Francisco, the WZMH Group of Dallas, and HGA as associate architects and engineers. Completed in 1987, the Radisson Plaza VII contained hotel space on the first 17 floors, with retailing located on the second floor skyway and 18 more stories of office space crowned with a gable roof.

In the heart of revitalized downtown Rochester, the new Radisson Centerplace Hotel gives the city another contemporary hotel for the multitudes of visitors seeking health care in the famous medical community. The hotel is linked by skyway to its retailing-office neighbor, Centerplace Galleria across the street, and to the Mayo Clinic subway system.

The Radisson University Hotel had to be sensitive to the surrounding campus while appealing to guests. The solution was to use a dark red brick and to maintain the scale of adjacent shops.

CHAPTER VIII

Gary Hall

Bob Parupsky

"Wired for Change," written by Gary Hall for *Architectural Technology* in 1984, describes how power distribution equipment set into the floor enables new and remodeled offices to meet changing demands of the latest technology.

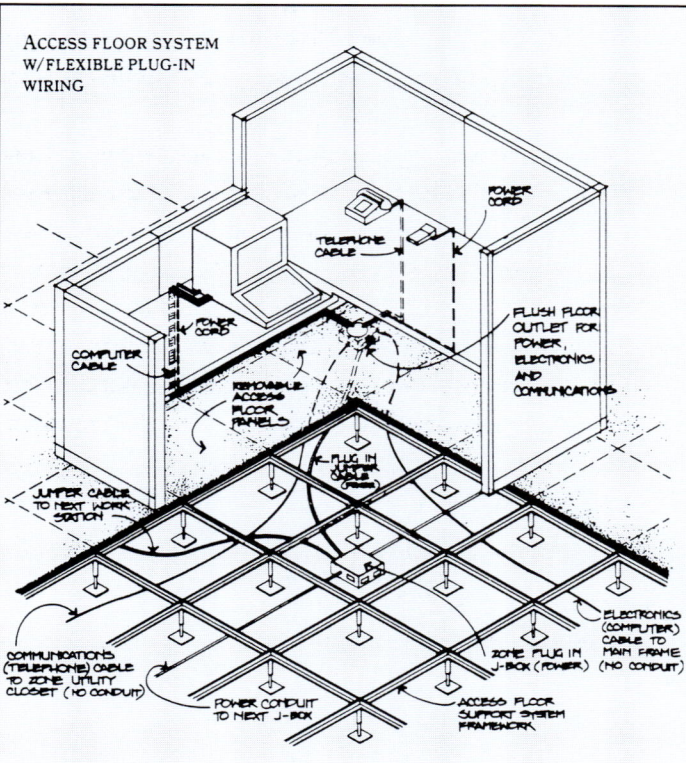

The World of High-Tech

As the world of high-tech accelerated in the 1980s, HGA engineers acquired more and more expertise and hired additional engineering specialists. For many clients, engineering — mechanical, electrical, structural, and civil — constituted up to 50 percent of a building's costs and there were new, more complex issues — electronics and telecommunications, computer and clean room environments, uninterrupted power systems, well water cooling, and contaminated site soil conditions. Hospital facilities, especially, required elaborate networks of complicated systems. The collaboration of engineers with architects, an HGA policy since its beginning, was now more important than ever.

Structural Engineering

In 1980 the firm established its first structural engineering department, headed by Jim Goulet and Jack Larson. For 27 years HGA had relied primarily on the consulting firm of Johnston-Sahlman Structural Engineers. "Architects make a thing of beauty, but engineers have to make it safe. Structural engineers have to have imagination and the ability to make something work without hindering the architects' ideas," said Milan Johnston. With Johnston and Sahlman's impending retirement, John Pearson became the main contact for the firm. With an increasing desire to have all engineering disciplines in-house, HGA started its own structural engineering department just before the move to Minneapolis.

In 1985 the group began to blossom under the leadership of David Galey, a Cornell University graduate and an accomplished structural engineer. Galey began building the department with skilled men and women working closely with the architects. "In structural engineering, there has to be a real marriage with the

> "Architects make a thing of beauty, but engineers have to make it safe."
> Milan Johnston

HAMMEL GREEN AND ABRAHAMSON

CHAPTER VIII

An aerial view of the new VA cafeteria

Structural engineering completed the "total engineering in house" concept.

Dave Galey

A dental office overlooking the atrium

architecture...It's a big responsibility, making a building safe. And it's especially challenging now because so many jobs are on fast track. Structural engineering is also a creative task; a matter of being able to give the architects various options," said Galey. The following year, the department implemented a variety of innovative techniques to strengthen the floors of the old Minneapolis City Hall. Other jobs in this 1890s structure followed.

The V.A. Hospital

In 1983 the engineering department faced one of its biggest challenges. When the massive new Veterans Administration Medical Center was topped off with the traditional evergreen tree in May 1985, a construction worker hung on it a bloodstained flag used by his uncle as a bandage in World War II. Veterans of the upper midwest appreciated that symbol on their new hospital, the largest project in the Veterans Administration history.

It was no secret that the old center was outmoded. A 1974 study showed that it was the worst in the national system — archaic bed wards, inadequate bathing facilities, no air conditioning, scattered departments, and out-of-date buildings. Regional V.A. officials began to take action, and in 1984 Congress came through with the necessary funding.

Word of the huge project spread throughout the building industry. At HGA, George Riches and his health care team put together a major joint venture involving HDR (Henningson, Durham & Richardson) of Omaha, Smiley-Glotter Associates of Minneapolis, and HGA, which by now had acquired a wealth of health care experience. The "MVA Group" was awarded the commission, and in the fall of 1981 it began work, taking over the lower floor of HGA's downtown Minneapolis office. The HGA team was

"When we were dealing with the county jail, the inmates were very helpful in pointing out new cracks in their cell spaces."
Dave Galey

CHAPTER VIII

To help visitors and patients find their way into the V.A. Medical Center, the architects planned a large main entrance, clearly defined by a linear canopy. Inside, a soaring four-story lobby complete with huge American flag, greets the visitor.

CHAPTER VIII

to design the building as well as be responsible for mechanical, electrical, and civil engineering systems.

Using a master plan developed previously, the designers were to bring under one roof all the medical functions scattered around the 132-acre campus and to provide 845 beds, 18 operating rooms, research labs, offices, cafeteria, chapel, support facilities, and auditorium, while visually minimizing the facility's size. One requirement was a window for every patient's room; if every window were to the outside, however, the hospital would be enormous; the architects suggested three sunny atriums to give patients daylight, greenery, and a sense of the outdoors. "We had to convince the V.A. that atriums could solve the problem and be built for the same cost," said project manager Jerry Olson. Airport height regulations meant that the hospital could be only five stories, so the brick and precast concrete building housing patient rooms had to sprawl over seven acres. Steel and paneled glass were chosen to enclose the clinic, office, and administrative wing.

The hospital required elaborate engineering: "It was an awesome structure from the mechanical point of view," said director of mechanical engineering Bob Parupsky. "With mechanical/electrical floors between each hospital floor — interstitial space — all the major pipes, conduits, and duct runs for electrical, heating, and plumbing systems are accessible." In 1987, HGA and HDR engineers accepted a "Seven Wonders of Engineering" award from the Minnesota Society of Professional Engineers.

By September 1987, the Minneapolis Veterans Administration Medical Center, the largest single construction project in Minnesota, was completed on time and under budget by M. A. Mortenson Company, general contractors. "The dedication was a milestone in the development of the V.A. system," said designer Kurt Rogness. "Having worked on it for three years and another three to build it, we felt very gratified to see it occupied."

H. B. Fuller Company's Willow Lake Research Laboratory

In 1980, an HGA design team took on the challenge of designing a chemical research lab on the edge of a small suburban lake and wildlife preserve in Vadnais Heights, Minnesota. H. B. Fuller Company, internationally known for its adhesives and specialty chemicals, requested that no fossil fuel be burned in the new facility; and because the site was a protected preserve, the designers made sure they did not harm the natural environment.

Team engineers were determined to incorporate all available technologies of energy conservation, while the architects

Natural light creates a balance between indoors and outdoors.

A dramatic lab entrance.

"Working for the government is always a pleasure."
HGA anonymous

Sheltered by earth on three sides, the H. B. Fuller Willow Lake Laboratory steps down to the lake. Window overhangs allow solar gain during winter and shade during summer. Insulated skylights admit daylight deep into the laboratory space, reducing heat loss and the need for artificial light.

CHAPTER VIII

were inspired to integrate energy-saving features by setting the building into the hillside overlooking the lake. Bill Anderson was principal, Loren Ahles was the designer, and the engineers were led by Jim Goulet, Gary Hall, and Harry Wilcox. Fred Dubin of Dubin-Boone Associates was energy management consultant.

Engineered for energy conservation, the lab is heated and cooled by water from the Jordan aquifer, 325 feet below ground. After the removal of heat, the water was stream-aerated and discharged to the once dying Willow Lake, now thriving with waterfowl. "Fuller's determination not to burn fossil fuels led to our use of well water as the source of energy," said Wilcox.

The Willow Lake lab captured a MSAIA merit award in 1982, a national energy award from ASHRAE in 1986, and an International Winter Cities Consortium award for excellence in responding to Minnesota's winter environment in 1988.

The Piper Jaffray Tower

HGA's first chance to design a speculative office tower came in 1982 when William Maddux decided to build the Piper Jaffray Tower with an all-Minnesota team. Michael Niemeyer, HGA principal, chanced to meet an associate of Maddux Properties at a local Porsche club event where he heard about the proposed tower. He quickly arranged to introduce Maddux to some of the other HGA principals. After learning of the firm's reputation for full-service architecture and engineering, Maddux chose HGA. Vice president Niemeyer became project principal, Bruce Abrahamson headed the design team, and Dennis Wallace was project manager. Architect Dae Min was one of the key contributors to the design. For engineering, Bob Kaczke led mechanical, Jim Moravek electrical, and Jim Goulet civil. The developer asked for a building with a professional image that

Rising to 42 stories, the Piper Jaffray Tower is a reflective beacon on the Minneapolis skyline. A blue and silver-colored curtain wall reflects sunlight while a steel shaft runs full height at one corner.

CHAPTER VIII

The design team in action

Warm Kasota stone at the base complements the green glass of Minnesota Center. The green tones provide continuity throughout the interior.

"looked like it belonged in the pinstriped community."

Excitement grew as an animated design team worked intently on the scheme of its first major office tower. The challenge was how to make a squat, bulky building soar. "We didn't want to do a traditional flat-topped design," said Niemeyer. The designers were influenced by the stepped corners of the IDS Tower and the tapering of the Foshay Tower. "We translated that into a stepped approach on a larger scale," he said.

Inside the tower, HGA engineers designed a distribution network allowing easy access for tenants on all 42 floors. All mechanical and electrical systems were electronically controlled, providing what the industry calls a "smart" building. An in-floor cellular system allowed tenant changes to be made quickly without intruding on other offices or on adjacent floors. Construction of the tower (named for lead tenant, the historic brokerage firm of Piper, Jaffray & Hopwood) was completed in 1984.

One Minnesota Center

HGA's next major tower project was for Homart Development Company, a nationally known commercial arm of Sears, Roebuck and Company. Homart had acquired acreage near I-494 in suburban Bloomington, with the intention of developing first a speculative office tower and, later, more offices and a luxury hotel.

Work on the office tower began in 1985 with Loren Ahles as project designer and Perry Bolin, principal. The red-headed Ahles, with a master's degree in architecture from MIT, had established himself as a creative force since joining the firm 10 years earlier. Other members of the Homart team included: project designer Bake Baker, project architect Dennis Wallace, and engineers Jim Moravek, John Bauch, Dick Peterson, and Jim Goulet.

"We shape our buildings and afterwards our buildings shape us."
Winston Churchill

CHAPTER VIII

According to Perry Bolin, it was important to strike a strong corporate image and bold signature on the skyline. "You perceive the building while going 60 miles an hour, so it had to be a kind of sculptural form to interest leasers," said Ahles. The design team's solution for Phase I combined two intersecting rectangles of differing widths in jade green reflective glass. The two towers, 13 and 15 stories high, had heated parking below and a unique floor plate allowing for a number of corner offices and virtually column-free space. In 1988, the structural system of Minnesota Center received an Minnesota Consulting Engineers Council grand award.

A unique feature of the Minnesota Center design was the exterior lighting outlining the top of the tower. Light pipes there change from lavender and pink to blue and green, depending on the season.

Phillips Plastics Corporate Center, Phillips, Wisconsin

In contrast with large-scale corporate projects, smaller office projects also came to HGA. The Phillips Plastics Corporation asked for a small but highly workable corporate headquarters that would fit into a rural Wisconsin setting of forest and lakeshore. An HGA design team led by project designer Julie Snow and principal Dennis Lanz used two hip-roofed pavilions of cedar and teak, plus lots of glass on the lakeshore facade, in a simple geometric form with a weathered copper roof.

The effectiveness of the Phillips Plastic Headquarters design was recognized with a MSAIA Honor Award in 1987.

CHAPTER VIII

And Now for Something Completely Different

HGA created pageantry at Canterbury Downs with turret buildings, checkered track markers, flying pennants, and gold ball "finials" on every red roof.

CHAPTER VIII

Canterbury Downs

In 1983, the Minnesota Legislature voted to allow pari-mutuel betting in the state and to establish a racing commission that would license a track for horseracing. Shortly thereafter, five separate development groups came forward with site proposals — all within easy driving distance of the Twin Cities. Excitement grew as competition quickened.

One developer began putting together a proposal for a Shakopee site it felt could not fail to win. This group called itself Minnesota Racetrack, Inc. (MRI), and included the following investors: Santa Anita Operating Company, North American Life and Casualty Company, Fidelity Union Life Insurance Company, Scotland, Inc., and two area businessmen, Brook Fields, Jr. and Brooks Hauser. MRI also put together a team it felt could "run the mile" — racetrack manager Santa Anita Companies of California and architect Ewing Cole Cherry Parsky of Philadelphia, which had designed many racetracks. In addition, the group wisely figured it needed a local architectural firm of high reputation and abilities for site planning and design of all support facilities.

Fields and Hauser began interviewing area architects. HGA vice president Michael Niemeyer had been quietly pursuing leads, learning as much as he could from an engineer friend who raced quarterhorses and, as it turned out, had already been contacted by the Shakopee group. A good friend of HGA's, the engineer recommended the company to the investment group. Dick Hammel and marketing director Riches went out for the initial interview. Though neither HGA nor any other firm in Minnesota had ever done a racetrack, the two established a rapport with MRI as "fellow Minnesota businessmen and gentlemen," recalled Riches. Soon afterwards, HGA was informed it had the job.

HGA was mainly responsible for designing the Canterbury Downs backstretch, a 70-acre village for jockeys, owners, and horses.

Over 400 grooms live in quarters distributed throughout 24 stables.

Canterbury Downs was the cover story for *AM* magazine.

"We learned a lot about horses and racing in just a few days."
Mike Niemeyer

CHAPTER VIII

The racetrack site controversy was now heating up. With prominent headlines and daily TV coverage, the racing commission finally voted. The Shakopee site won! The elated architects celebrated with their clients that evening, and a design team was quickly organized with Michael Niemeyer as principal, Loren Ahles as project designer, Nancy Stark as project manager, and Jim Goulet as civil engineer, working with Kraus Anderson contractors. The huge project had to be ready in 16 months.

Chief civil engineer Goulet took special pride in the Minnesota racetrack. "The civil development was massive in scope, and very diverse — the retention ponds, the relative variation of geological contact, the porous soil overlying a major aquifer, the sewerage network and water distribution, plus irrigation." Goulet's team did all the civil work and designed a track widely recognized as having the best running surface in the nation.

In developing the site plan on what once was prairie country, the architects recalled English horseracing traditions. "We used baroque planning concepts and purposely made use of long vistas, axes, and monuments to help visitors orient themselves," said Ahles. The site was divided into two separate areas — the grandstand for public movement and the backstretch for trainers and grooms. As trumpets announced the start of the first race in June 1985, fans flocked to the paddock outside the grandstand. "And now they're off!" had a special meaning for HGA architects and engineers watching the thoroughbreds and their jockeys pull away from the starting gate.

Canterbury Downs opened its gates only 16 months after the start of design development drawings. For project manager Nancy Stark, it was a whirlwind balancing act to coordinate the work of two different design teams, multiple engineering groups, and two sets of owners. In 1986, it won a MSAIA Honor Award. In 1988, Stark became an associate vice president.

"You don't get a racetrack every day."
George Riches

CHAPTER ~ IX

Lloyd skelton Roxanne lange Saint mary's cathedral Tom hamill Sandy robinson Ceal tennent Judy gilchrist Dave arkin Dave zenk Kurt putnam Kim dahlson Saint mary's of the lake Mollie schleisman Ed towey Bill lent Darrell brinkman William kissinger Gerry mussetter Jennifer goldman husman Lincoln hotels Debbie edwards Keith hoy Ella kogan Scott johnson Tom larson Mike granucci Jason hagen Jefferson companies Kurt liebenow Larry opseth Joan soranno Tracey jacques Barb maguire Heidi myers Cheryl bond Maddux properties Janet whitmore Charles furness Harold jacobson Nick howard Melinda seymour Franc strgar James parsons Carlson companies Cindy huber Tina sabby Sheryl haefer Mara lynn mercer Dawn walters James seeks Cindy gipple Embassy suites Keith jacobson Mark noel Amie ferguson Sean phillips Connie wexler Duane johnson Jeff urmann City of minneapolis Pam harwood Doug fell Nancy joseph Jerry worrell

Carol prigge Tom oslund Sami karam Veterans administration Kermit olson Wayne clarke Gerry mussetter Ron kurtz Scott olsen John blum Patrick ballou H.B. fuller Susan newhall Lauren wold James ziegler Scott stangeland Eric glans Jon stumpf Ron powell Homart development company Betty forslund Marcia jergenson Doug pearson Judy kline Denise tennen Gail manning Phillips plastics corporation Jo anderson Lea musolf Mary beth marhoefer Lisa friedlander Bob gavin John clarey Bob lundgren Minnesota racetrack, inc. Tom oliphant Lauri harms Terry tangedahl Dana widstrom Don roberts Claudia jondahl Ron brustad Minnesota historical society Jim keans Tony mills Kent davidson Bruce clark Kurt putnam Simone l'heureux Kevin wargin Tom peterson Tim carlson Peter rauma

CHAPTER IX

NEW LANDMARKS FOR THE MIDWEST

The home-town team wins the national competition!

Traditional architectural elements presented in a classic watercolor format

Minnesota History Center design team.

In a 1987 design statement, Bruce Abrahamson wrote: "Good architecture, as well as having freshness, should have dignity, a sense of history, and solidity." Other HGA designers echoed that theme, saying they strive to create architecture that is timeless, not trendy or faddish. A good example of this philosophy is the Minnesota History Center project won by HGA in a national competition in 1986.

The Minnesota History Center

Founded in 1849, the Minnesota Historical Society (MHS) had been housed in a classic Greek Revival building next to the Capitol since 1917. By the early 1980s the Society had long outgrown its space, scattering its myriad functions around the state. It asked the Legislature for an addition to its existing building, and in 1984, after much debate, the Legislature determined that the old MHS structure should become part of the new Minnesota Judicial Center and that the Historical Society should have its own new headquarters. In December 1985, the Miller Hospital property across Interstate 94 from the Capitol mall became the site for a new Minnesota History Center, and the old hospital was demolished.

Meanwhile, a national design competition, sponsored by the Capitol Area Architectural and Planning Board and juried by nationally known architects and state officials, was underway. At HGA project designer Loren Ahles, project manager Gary Reetz, and principal Bruce Abrahamson set up "History Central", recruiting 11 teams from all departments. Entries were strictly anonymous, with more than 100 prestigious firms from around the country submitting proposals. The only all-Minnesota team among the six finalists, HGA was notified in June 1986 that its L-shaped design had won. The firm's founders, especially, were excited when a younger partner, designer Loren Ahles, accepted the award. "HGA's design was a remarkably detailed response to our very specific and complicated program," said Nina Archabal, later Director of the MHS.

The winning design solved the problem of a hillside site — overlooking the city of St. Paul, the Capitol, and the St. Paul Cathedral — soon to become an island wedged between freeways. "We

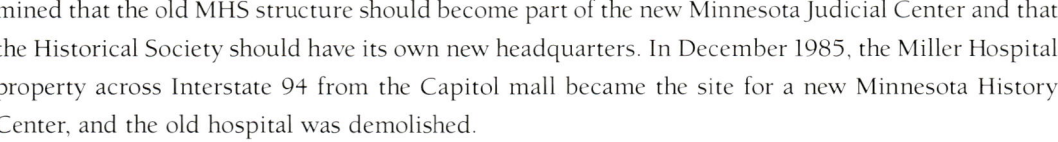

"Winning reinforces our belief in the way we design."
Bruce Abrahamson

CHAPTER IX

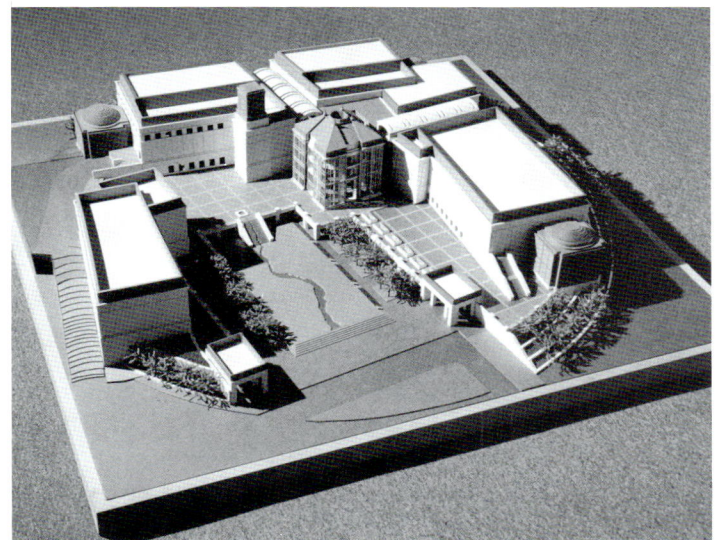

HGA's concept for the Minnesota History Center was an L-shaped, six-level structure, expansive like the midwestern prairie country but with formal granite and limestone facades reflecting the classic dignity of the Capitol and St. Paul Cathedral. A grand arcade punctuates the broad curving north facade.

CHAPTER IX

wanted to keep the articles of Minnesota's history safe, yet show them off," Ahles said. "Our idea was to create a big safe house for history with welcoming public areas."

In the design, the courtyard and main entrance are dominated by the copper-roofed Great Hall, a glass atrium from which visitors can reach exhibitions, reference rooms, and other services. Indigenous building materials, including Minnesota granite and limestone, were selected for the exterior. For the terraced courtyard facing downtown St. Paul, HGA landscape designer Tom Oslund selected Minnesota trees such as birch and maple. A central fountain and works of public art complete the landscaping. The courtyard serves as a public pedestrian link to the historic Summit Avenue neighborhood. The new building, slated for completion by 1991, will house not only the Society's extensive archival collections, but also a library, a museum, educational facilities, and administrative offices as well as a museum shop, restaurant, and other public amenities.

With the award of the Minnesota History Center commission, HGA again demonstrated that museum and fine arts facilities design is one of its strong points. The design teams' efforts have resulted in award-winning college centers for studio and performing arts, music theaters, secondary school auditoriums, and many space theaters for science museums across the country. Two favorite projects included the remodeling of the Jemne Building in St. Paul, home of the Minnesota Museum of Art's permanent collection, and the expansion of Walker Art Center in Minneapolis. Working with Edward Larabee Barnes and Museum Director Martin Friedman, HGA doubled the Walker's space. HGA is also working with the Minneapolis Institute of Arts in an evolving program of building improvements.

Facing HGA's largest, most complex secondary school design ever, the design team came up with this U-shaped, classically symmetrical form for the Eagan High School and Dakota Hills Middle School, linking both schools with a bright common lobby that overlooks an expansive courtyard.

"We're charting new territory here. There are only three other high schools in the whole country like this one,"
Principal Tom Wilson

HAMMEL GREEN AND ABRAHAMSON

CHAPTER IX

Eagan High School and Dakota Hills Middle School

HGA architects, who over 35 years have planned schools with top educators in diverse school districts, are witnessing a third wave of increasing enrollment in some school districts. Owatonna, one of the first districts calling on Hammel and Green 34 years ago, again commissioned the firm for projects in 1988. Changing technology drives much of the new work, according to principal Dan Swedberg. "Media expansion and computer center needs have forced updating in many districts. Computer technology is an integral part of elementary education."

Rosemount School District #196, in particular, has in the past 30 years given HGA the chance to excel in school design. Minnesota had not seen the construction of a new high school for almost a decade, according to Thomas Wilson (Principal on special assignment in charge of Eagan schools), until the Rosemount School District's population mushroomed. A bond issue authorizing both a high school and a middle school in Eagan passed late in 1987. Design began immediately.

Since the District already owned 116 acres next to an Eagan city park, it made economic sense to build both schools on the same site. In a unique partnership, the City of Eagan and the School District agreed to share outdoor athletic facilities on approximately 90 acres of land where tennis courts, track, baseball, football, and soccer fields could be used by all.

Both schools had to be vast (1,200 students in each, expandable to 2,000 in the high school) and technologically advanced. Certain facilities like the theater, instructional technical center (ITC), kitchen, and heating and cooling plants, could be shared by the schools. The Middle School had to include a competition-style swimming pool and diving well plus a warehouse area serving the entire school district.

Designing a project of such scope required many programming meetings with Superintendent R. J. "Red" Rehwaldt, Tom Wilson, other administrators, faculty, and school board members. Kurt Rogness was principal, with Ted Rozeboom project manager, Ted Butler senior project designer, Tom Johnson project designer, Bruce Jilk project architect, Laurie Parriott interior designer, Jim Moravek electrical engineer, and Jim Husnik civil engineer.

"Eagan is a high school for the next century," said Jim Moravek, who became an HGA vice president in 1989, "the most technologically advanced secondary school in the Midwest." In describing the school's technology, he explained that a coaxial cable system forms communication pathways, allowing transmission of voice, data, and video signals to each classroom, with channels to spare. Through a simple telephone switch, the path-

The Eagan High School design team at the construction site.

Deerwood Elementary was the first primary school in the district with two levels. Programmed for 750 K-5 students, it also housed classrooms for preschoolers and emotionally and behaviorally disturbed children.

The school won a 1988 MSAIA award for HGA's design team — Kurt Rogness, Ted Rozeboom, and Ted Butler.

CHAPTER IX

ways could tie in classroom computers with other computers anywhere in the world. "This technology is novel for a high school," said Moravek. The heart of the new building, shared by both schools, is the ITC, with a completely equipped TV studio for students and access to extensive computer and voice-data systems.

Paul Williams

The entire school is wired for video and computer access. According to Wilson, "Since the last three generations have been raised on TV, they have come to expect that fast pace as the norm. No teacher can match that. With VCRs, TV sets, and computer access in every classroom, we are empowering teachers a lot, and it affects the teaching/learning process enormously. Instead of waiting for the future to happen, we're creating it in Eagan." Dakota Hills Middle School is scheduled for a fall 1989 opening, with completion of Eagan High School slated for January 1990.

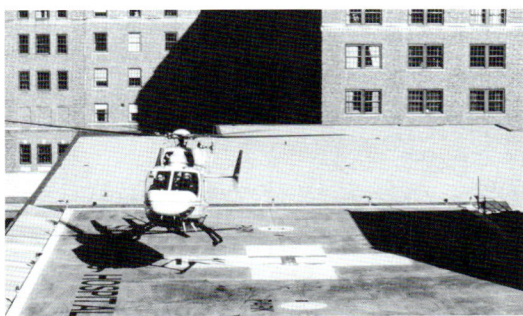

Trauma patients can now be treated with increasing effectiveness.

The Mayo Clinic

HGA's first project with Mayo in 1982 was a radiology and cardiology imaging center at Saint Marys Hospital. Next came two remodeling projects for research and outpatient laboratories, followed by physical medicine and rehabilitative services in 1983 and 1984. HGA also began a campus master facility plan for Saint Marys in 1984; this plan has been constantly updated to reflect current changes in medical practices, efficient facilities utilization and future improvements in pediatrics, pharmacy, med/surgical nursing, cardiac services and intensive care.

A rooftop heliport was designed for Saint Marys in 1985, allowing quick access to the emergency trauma unit. The new helipad and hangar became home for a medically configured twin-engine BK 117 "spaceship", heart of the first hospital-based helicop-

The Mayo Clinic opened a new telemedicine facility in 1987.

HAMMEL GREEN AND ABRAHAMSON

CHAPTER IX

ter transport program in Minnesota. A major merger took place in 1987 when Saint Marys and Methodist hospitals merged with the Mayo Clinic to form the Mayo Medical Center. In 1988, a state-of-the-art 1.5 Tesla transportable and two 1.5 Tesla site-built MRI (magnetic resonance imaging) facilities were completed.

Paul Williams, one of the firm's principal medical specialists said, "Because some of our staff work on health care constantly, they become so specialized that their knowledge is invaluable. That's the key to building our whole medical practice. We're constantly growing in that knowledge, yet we have the experience to look back and learn from it." Medical planner Gary Nyberg added, "The new technology is a significant part of our business — intensive care units, cardiac surgery, heart and lung transplant operations, magnetic energy scanning, and birthing rooms. We learn right along with our clients."

HGA's team of health care specialists continues to provide design services for Saint Marys from architecture and engineering to interior design to planning. Just as medical technology leapfrogs into the future, so must the firm's health care teams.

The Harold W. Siebens Medical Education Building

When HGA was asked to design a new education building for Mayo on a site adjacent to the historic Plummer Building, designers took a deep breath. The Plummer Building has been a Rochester landmark since it was built in 1928. Topped with a terra cotta belfry, the 15-story building is Neo-Gothic in style. What was the appropriate architectural response to the call for a modern high-rise center offering education and telecommunications programs? With principal Jerry Olson and designer Bruce Abrahamson, the team chose both materials and form to link the two.

The Mayo teleconference center was designed as a sophisticated television studio where Mayo Clinic staff can transmit and receive live conferences.

HAMMEL GREEN AND ABRAHAMSON

CHAPTER IX

The interior was designed by HGA engineers to support state-of-the-art technology. Here the Mayo Medical Center can develop and broadcast medical programs to TV networks everywhere. Teleconferencing facilities allow physicians at Mayo's satellite clinics to confer regularly with their colleagues in Rochester and give medical students access to videotaped seminars. The concourse level was planned as a new focus for Mayo's renowned pedestrian subway system. There, in an underground patient lounge, a three-story atrium filled with daylight and indoor greenery would give patients a place to relax. The stately structure, to be completed in late 1989, is named for its major contributor, Harold W. Siebens, a leading Canadian benefactor.

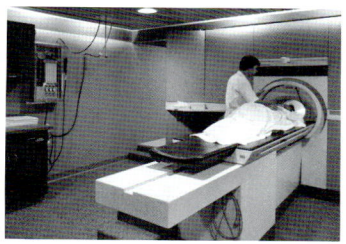

The new MRI facility exemplifies Mayo's commitment to medical innovation.

Other Hospitals

As HGA's medical specialization grows, the firm finds itself working with hospitals in other cities and states — Appleton, La Crosse, Milwaukee, and Madison, Wisconsin; the Detroit area and Iron Mountain, Michigan; Peoria and Springfield, Illinois; Cincinnati, Ohio; Fargo, North Dakota; Pierre, South Dakota; and Cheyenne, Wyoming. The health care team also works on many major Twin Cities hospital projects such as a transplant intensive care unit at Abbott Northwestern and an ICU at Metropolitan Medical Center. In 1989, a substantial design challenge came from United and Children's Hospital of St. Paul — to create an Ambulatory Care Center with character and identity in the midst of a complex hospital campus. Dennis Lanz was named managing principal, with design principal Dan Avchen, project designer Vince James, and medical planner Ted Rozeboom on the team.

In 1985, HGA joined an eastern team for the massive enlargement of Massachusetts General Hospital in Boston, a

Mayo's new educational facility has a warm stone base that echos the sandstone of the Plummer Building. The mass stepped back, so it did not block its neighbor's windows and grey curtainwall was chosen to reflect its intricate ornamentation. A solarium capped the structure with a form reminiscent of the Plummer Building's crown.

"We searched for an appropriate image reflecting the pre-eminence and world class stature of Mayo."
Bruce Abrahamson

CHAPTER IX

When the Minnetonka Community Center opened in 1987, it quickly attracted young and old alike. As Curt Green saw the project reach completion, he expressed satisfaction in the "daylight, color, logic and visual charisma" that emerged as a result of his design.

project in which it associated with Hoskins Scott Taylor of Boston. To handle this assignment, an entire design team including Nancy Stark, Don Wong, Gary Nyberg, Bob Lundgren, Joseph DeRosier, and Katie Kiefer went to Boston for two years.

HGA architects and engineers specializing in health care facilities find much personal gratification in the work. Principal Paul Williams is one. Williams said, "Designing a hospital is like designing a small community. The design solutions require an important merger of function with design. I find that a very creative challenge."

The Minnetonka Community Center

When the City of Minnetonka, a Minneapolis suburb, awarded HGA the commission to design an addition to the community center, Curt Green welcomed the assignment because of its unique site near Minnehaha Creek, marshes and woodlands. Minnetonka wanted the new community center to be integrated with its master plan and to connect with city hall. It was to contain city council chambers, civic group spaces, and facilities for a senior center.

With principal designer Green and project manager Gary Reetz, the design team set to work. The city's plan developed a large holding pond in front to set off the center from a widely traveled road. The building exterior had to conform conceptually to the existing dark red brick city hall, so the architects matched the brick but introduced accents of Minnetonka blue and added a new peaked copper roof to recall the original building. "Because it was a place for the community to gather, we used lots of glass to bring natural light into the public spaces," said Reetz. An L-shaped skylight divides the council chambers from the support offices.

"We are a young team with mature ideas."
Dick Hammel, Curt Green and Bruce Abrahamson in the 50s.

"We are a mature team with young ideas."
Said the three in the 80s.

Roger Santelman

HGA's design for the Minneapolis Main Post Office enhanced the city's plan for development of the riverfront. The scheme shows a grand pedestrian stairway to the river, complete with lower-level arcade for future retail spaces.

Minneapolis Post Office

The needs of government, the impact on the environment, the public demand for more pleasing cityscapes — all are issues frequently faced by architects and engineers working with civic clients. When the Minneapolis Main Post Office selected HGA in 1987 to design a major addition to its existing art deco building, it was confronted with all three issues. The post office overlooks the Mississippi River and the Falls of St. Anthony, where the Minneapolis Park Board had recently completed a beautiful parkway. The Postal Service also wanted to retain the architectural integrity of its 1933 Kasota stone facility. "The post office expansion was very controversial because the City, Park Board and Minneapolis Community Development Agency (MCDA) were all at odds with one another on the right approach to take," said HGA principal Roger Santelman. "We took on a facilitator role and after many meetings came up with a solution everyone was happy with." In the design solution, Santelman, with designer Loren Ahles and project architect Steve Miller, repeated the simple volumes and streamlined detailing of the original building in the new processing facility, while closely reflecting its Art Deco heritage. The Minneapolis Main Post Office addition is scheduled for completion in 1991.

USDA Research Building, Northern Crop Science Laboratory

The U.S. Department of Agriculture (USDA) needed a new crop research building at North Dakota State University in Fargo. It would house a community of scientists, faculty, and students in high-tech labs for the study of northern crops such as wheat, sunflowers, and sugarbeets, as well as provide a special environment for the University's electron microscope equipment. The new

"HGA is willing to work stylistically across boundaries."
Gary Reetz

CHAPTER IX

The Northern Crop Science Laboratory for the USDA won a 1988 MSAIA award for the ingenuity of its design.

CHAPTER IX

Dennis Lanz

facility would be attached to existing greenhouses.

Several considerations — the northern prairie landscape just beyond the campus, the traditions of the family farm, and diverse technological and functional requirements — influenced the design team led by principal Dennis Lanz, project manager Greg Haley, and designers Loren Ahles and Steve Miller. The team developed an architecture reminiscent of a farmstead, complete with silo and peaked roofs. The most daring feature was a bold silo-shaped space housing a spiral staircase connecting the two floors. Post-Modern design elements included a blue-green metal pitched roof and a brick course pattern for the exterior, with dark brick at the bottom and lighter brick at the top.

The "clerestory", an upper story often used for ventilation in barns, ran along the electron microscope suite bringing light to the preparation area. Underneath the pitched roof was space for mechanical equipment. For a contemporary touch, the lobby was of gray-tinted glass with copper-colored frames to be enjoyed from the staff lounge, conference room, and offices. The USDA lab, standing in contrast to other flat-topped campus buildings, was the subject of some controversy. Designer Steve Miller said: "We feel we celebrated agriculture and made a positive image that reflects what's going on inside — agricultural research."

U of M Electrical Engineering/Computer Science Building

When the State Designer Selection Board notified Hammel late in 1984 that HGA had been awarded the new U of M Electrical Engineering/Computer Science Building, he was particularly pleased. (Hammel had served on the Institute of Technology Board and in 1977 had received the University's Outstanding Achievement Award.) A top-flight design team was immediately

The main entry plaza opens to an exterior courtyard known as the U of M IT rotunda, forming the vibrant core of IT's campus.

Because the seven-level building has three floors underground, the architects used a greenhouse wall slanting upwards to bring natural light into all levels. Bright red trim accents the glass, while yellow and blue ducts appear on the roof.

"That building has my name on it."
Dick Hammel

CHAPTER IX

set up, with lead principal Hammel, designer Abrahamson, managing principal Duane Blanchard, and chief engineer Harry Wilcox. All worked closely with the IT Dean, E. F. Infante, Associate Dean Gordon Beaver, and with Robert Collins, Head of the Electrical Engineering School, and David Fox, Head of Computer Science at the U of M.

The design team's mission was to build a showplace for the IT. It had to be a dynamic building providing a new heart for the IT campus, while relating well to the surrounding brick and stone-clad older U of M buildings. The interior had to meet the rapidly changing nature of technology yet remain a pleasant learning place. Confronting these challenges, the designers responded boldly. "The building tries to communicate in three languages — the classic old one, a language in transition, and one that talks about the future," said Abrahamson. To provide more interest to the classic wall, the architects chose a horizontal banding pattern that changes from stone and brick to a combination of glazed black brick and the brick of adjoining buildings. Built on a small site, 40 percent of the structure is underground.

The building serves the teaching and research needs of the Electrical Engineering and Computer Science Departments. "The micro-electronics area is unique in that it had to be a near-vibration-free environment. Dealing with the production of micro-electronic chips requires an absolutely clean environment so the rooms are built at a standard of near purity of air conditions," said Blanchard about the building's technological requirements. More than 20 of HGA's brightest engineers, many of whom were U of M graduates, worked on the IT project with considerable satisfaction. In the fall of 1988, the new facility, constructed on a fast-track system, opened on schedule for students and faculty.

CHAPTER IX

NSP Transformer Maintenance Facility and Central Stores

In 1987, HGA was awarded its first heavy industrial commission. Northern States Power Company (NSP), a major utility company in the upper midwest, challenged the firm to design an industrial building on a new site in Maple Grove for the repair and refurbishing of electrical transformers up to 110 tons, and to build a connected central material supply facility. Principal Roger Santelman, working with Jerry Johnson and Lauren Wold, headed the design team.

Since the site was 20 feet above an aquifer in Maple Grove (prime source of municipal water for Maple Grove and nearby communities), of special design concern was the prevention of soil and water contamination resulting from accidental spillage of oil contained in the transformers. Chief civil engineer Jim Goulet and his team created a five-acre surface and underground containment system protecting the area from potential contaminants. "We appeared before the local Planning Commission and City Council four or five times to explain how this would work," said Goulet. (The repaired transformers would be filled only with pure mineral oil to further diminish the potential of contamination.)

For structural engineer Yanak Shagalov, the challenge was to design a transformer repair high-bay area for bridge cranes handling massive loads. Inside the repair building resembling a European train shed, huge overhead cranes would convey the transformers on tracks. "We had to determine the load capacity of this new equipment and make the building accept such a load," said Shagalov, whose background in industrial design comes from his training in Minsk in the Soviet Union. (Shagalov and his family have become American citizens since he joined the firm in 1981.)

3M

Attracted by the firm's team approach and close working relationships with clients, Roger Santelman brought a wealth of experience in corporate architecture when he joined HGA in 1984. "Here you get to know your client and experience the highs and lows of the project. That's the fun of it," Santelman said. Over the years, he had worked with 3M on a wide variety of projects. In the fall of 1988, he and his design team won a big one for HGA — a major health care products division office building at the 3M Center in St. Paul.

As the first significant building for 3M in Minnesota in ten years, the design concept had to respond to a new 3M corporate philosophy. That is, an entire division's staff, from management to research labs, sales, and marketing, would all be grouped in close proximity to each other to achieve improved communication, both

The new NSP Transformer Maintenance Facility fit well into the surrounding community thanks to extensive landscaping and earth berming. Blue and green accents the buff/grey masonry building. The 300,000 square foot building contains numerous support areas.

"Our engineers will do anything for a corporate client. Doug Fell went all out when he dove into a reservoir to inspect cracking in its basin."
Harry Wilcox

HAMMEL GREEN AND ABRAHAMSON

CHAPTER IX

formal and informal.

Leading the HGA design team were principal Roger Santelman, designer Abrahamson, engineering coordinator Jim Moravek, and interior programmer Nancy Cameron. To meet the schedule, the office beefed up its staff, adding 30 new people and for five to six months the 3M team worked on schematic and design development drawings.

Then came the call that every architectural office dreads. "Sorry," said the client's operating committee head, "But we must put this project on hold for six months." Team morale dropped. Fiscal projections became worrisome. The office struggled to regroup. One month later another call came — "Put the project back on schedule." Such is the up and down nature of the architectural business. The team resumed contract documents of the original scheme.

Sited between two existing lab buildings at the 3M Center, the new structure is clad in warm-toned brick to harmonize with its neighbors. To visually reduce the scale of the addition, designers divided the building with a soaring 7½-story glass atrium. A commons area with conference center, training rooms, auditorium, shops, and other support areas is located on the ground level of this atrium. Glass-enclosed pedestrian walkways connect the office complex to the adjacent buildings and to a sunny new cafeteria overlooking a small lake. An open courtyard separates the offices from the cafeteria creating what landscape designer Tom Oslund describes as a "visual oasis containing two gardens with plantings selected to resemble the 3M plaid."

Our Lady of Grace Catholic Church, Edina

After a survey of long-term needs, Our Lady of Grace Catholic Church in Edina decided to expand its Georgian colonial complex in 1984 by converting the old church into a gymnasium for its elementary school and building a major addition for a new church and other services. HGA won the commission in a three-

A major new office complex for 3M Center.

CHAPTER IX

firm competition. Design guru Ted Butler worked with principal Curt Green, project manager John Justus, and lighting designer Carol Chaffee.

This design team achieved a singular work of architecture in an open worship space, utterly simple and contemplative. Setting off the vaulted ceiling were deeply cut dormers and an open cupola. Seating for 1,100 around three sides of the altar created a sense of community. An arched colonnade or ambulatory, somewhat like a monk's cloister walk, borders the worship space and opens it to the outdoors. Numerous windows flood the room with light.

Connecting the new with the old, a concourse led to a skylit commons area. A new chapel, large meeting/dining room, kitchen, and several other rooms were included in the addition. Exterior architecture blended with the old through matching soft mud brick and Mankato stone; a hipped copper roof completed the Georgian colonial style.

Colonial Church of Edina Expansion

By 1985, crowding was again a problem at Colonial Church of Edina. Under Reverend Arthur Rouner's leadership, the church voted to finance another major addition. Hammel and Ted Butler were pleased to continue their plan for a complete New England village by adding three clapboard buildings for group activities, another fireplace room, study rooms, youth areas, counseling space, and a gymnasium, all connected with wide outward-looking "streets". They also finished the courtyard outside the meeting house with an intimate landscape garden, planned in true colonial style by HGA landscape designer Tom Oslund, as an arbor with native trees and flowers. Major modifications of the site included re-shaping the reflecting pond to give way for building expansion. To direct people across the pond to the new building, Butler created a New England-style covered bridge using traditional trusswork for the span. This expansion plan for Colonial Church turned out to be Hammel's last work.

The striking simplicity of Our Lady of Grace Church won three awards for HGA: a MSAIA Honor Award in 1987, a CEC Merit Award for innovative lighting, and a 1988 Interior Design Award from the MSAIA.

The natural environment of Our Lady of Grace provides a contemplative setting.

"For me, working on religious architecture is like giving my personal testimony."
John Justus

In a moving ceremony late in 1988, the Reverend Arthur Rouner, Larry Laukka, and other leaders of the Colonial Church of Edina dedicated the covered bridge, symbol of the finished Puritan village, in memory of their architect, Richard Hammel.

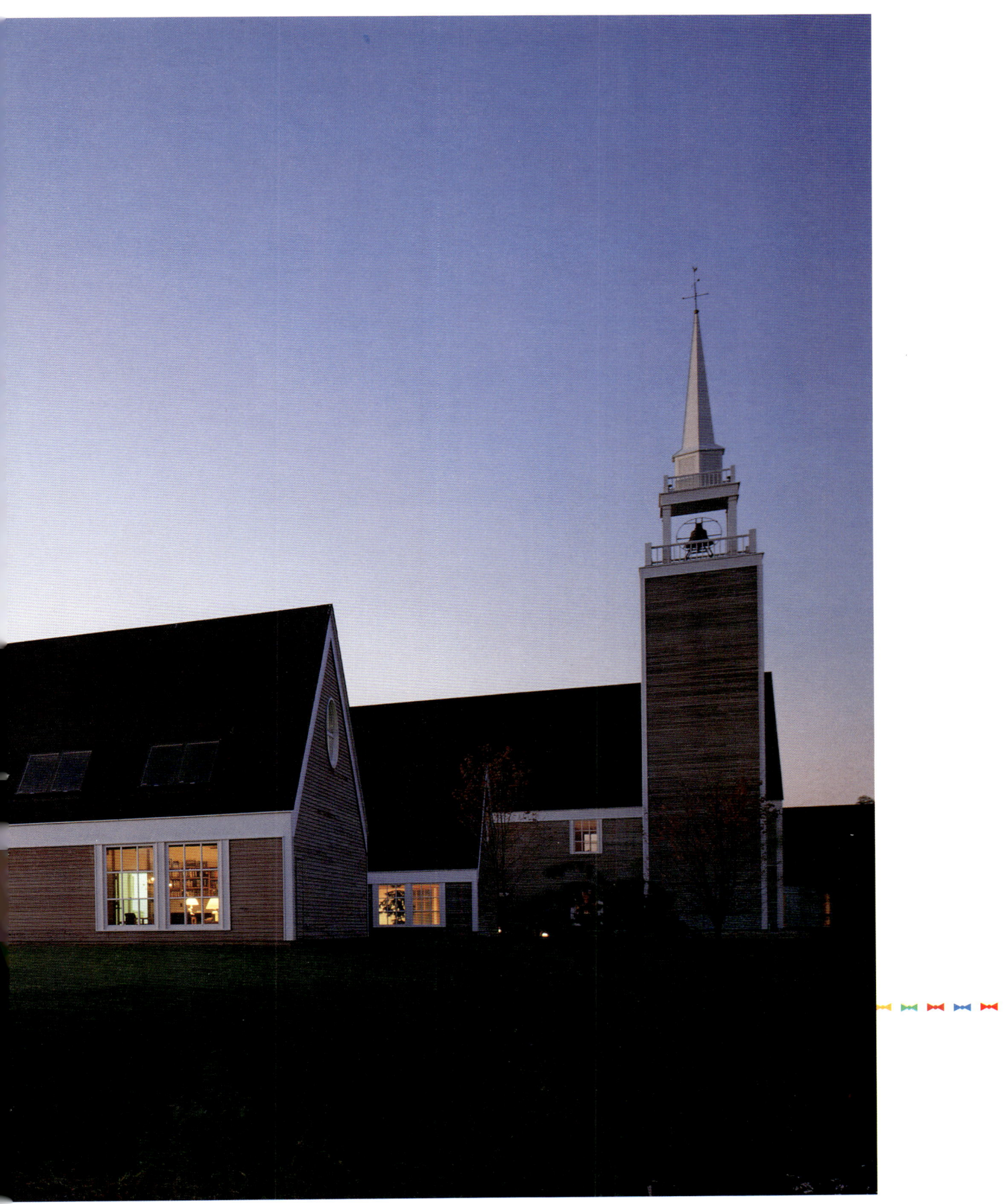

CHAPTER IX

The Death of Richard Hammel

Within a few short weeks after the fall meeting with Reverend Arthur Rouner, Larry Laukka, Ann Carrier, and other members of the Colonial Church building committee, Hammel was diagnosed with cancer of the lymph nodes. He suddenly became very ill and died November 18, 1986. His illness was complicated by a congenital circulatory problem that had left him without the sight of one eye and with a dangerous protruding condition in the other. Hammel never allowed this visual handicap to interfere with his life (except perhaps once in a sailboat race when he and his crew ran into the judge's boat!) In many ways, he ran his life as he did his sailboat — swiftly, meeting all challenges; confidently, asserting his pride in the firm; intelligently, making decisions and plans; and most of all, gently, treating all the people in his life with great good humor.

Hammel was only 63 when he died, just beginning to let go of the reins, and realizing what he, Green and Abrahamson had started 33 years before. "Who'd a' thunk it!" he remarked to Green while reviewing the annual report three weeks before his death.

On November 19, HGA president George Riches called a shocked staff together for a tribute to the man who had always taken the time to listen to everyone. Architectural technician Bill Kokotovich said: "Always it was Richard of the inciseful mind. There was a Zorba-like quality to him — adventuresome, innovative, a drive for growth. A twinkle of mischief was never too distant. Encompassing all of this was this man's sense of humor. Laughter was so much a real part of Richard Hammel, for me probably his most shining."

A deeply saddened crowd of more than a thousand relatives and friends, partners and staff, clients, business, civic and educational leaders attended his funeral that day in the simple beauty of Colonial Church. The Reverend Arthur Rouner spoke movingly of his friend, the church's architect, who had touched so many lives. Then in the hush, Hammel's lifelong partner, Curt Green, spoke: "While we may not have 'thunk' it 33 years ago, the leadership, intellect, and force from Dick gave us the inspiration to move upward and onward. For all of us at HGA, Dick created a bond upon which we built friendship, loyalty to our profession, and stature among our colleagues. All of us sorely miss his being here, but we will preserve the positive HGA spirit he left us with."

In the fall of 1987, Minnesota architects eloquently expressed their loss by voting to honor Hammel with the MSAIA Gold Medal Award for architectural excellence. The honor, never before given posthumously, has been awarded only five times earlier in the state.

Dick Hammel at work.

"Whenever Dick clarified his position on an issue, he would insert the name Fred Schmerz. We all assumed it to be a figure of speech. But after Dick's death, it was discovered that he was the Owatonna Registrar who recorded Hammels' birth."
Duane Blanchard

CHAPTER – X

Joel pearson Mark hansen Todd mohagen James brandt (duffy) The mayo clinic Denise joseph Ricardo cheng Mark ryan Wally johnson Paul swanson Jaye kirven Ron behnke Dana murdoch David reich Johanna hartman John harris Jill johnson Mart hatten Maria engebretson Troy tillman David jensen Lisa stenger Lisa tranby Roxanne lenzen George eklund Shun miyagi William fay David thorsen Allen kretman Mary battles Michael malone Wynne mattila Elizabeth crawford James parrish Paul taylor Carol neustel Petrice anderson Paul neseth Nadezhda podolskaya Allan wirth hammer Bobbie murray peterson Cliff jones doerr Vic pechaty Jim Jeff hancox Diane stre skow Nancy cameron

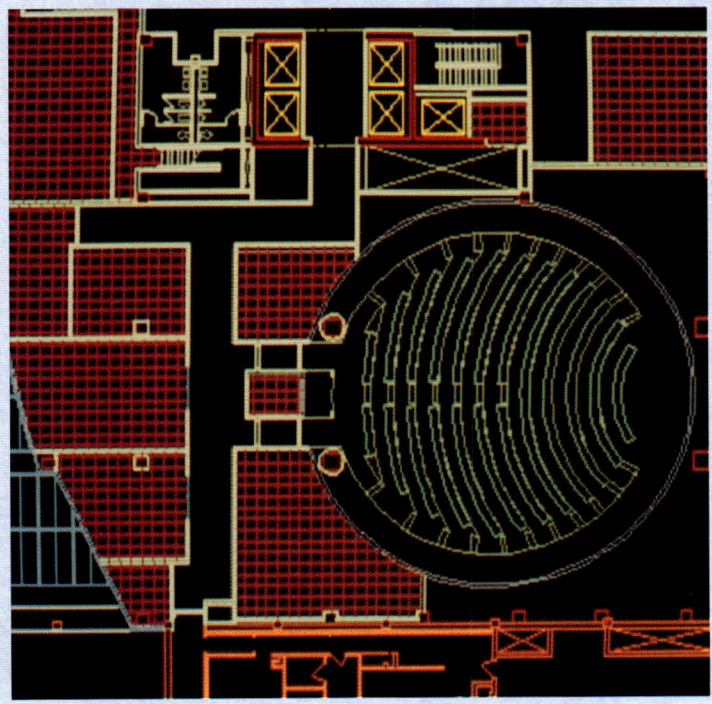

dosh Tim fairbanks Jeff Susan harris Tom lind Haidee tan Janet bur Tawnya stewart Ron Jack douthitt Howard Ed studniski William shields Diane watson low Greg haik Rob Robert jensen Robyn

manthe Phillip jackson Fred nicora Mike shewmaker Annette hanson Mike king Diana english Alissa williams Julie wilcox Mia kurtti Diana shagalov Chad omon Anthony eskridge Matt howd Brandi byrne Fred brechlin Pamela murawski Kelle donohue Laurie scheer 3M Steve makredes Dan yant Kathe flynn Glen johnson Hope wedge Mark cotroneo Craig anding Our lady of grace catholic church Mark reilly Rick hombsch Mary opila Nancy schumann Dave leschak Jeff hansen John montgomery Diana pachkofsky Kerry moore Catherine liska Dan mccormick Mike burgoyne Sue lunde Jennifer yoos Ann ellenberger Bob feyereisen Laura collins Michelle klein Bill peters Jamie pojek Lynda olander Dan pellinen Alex hering Sue harris Jerry helland Cherie claussen Cinda chorski Margaret larson Ron strandlund Peggy withrow Pat provinski Tom johnston Carmen delgado Randy lueth Joel zwier Carl dominguez Paul garvey Michael otubushin Jeffrey sebeck George benik Kate vermeland

CHAPTER X

CHAPTER X

LOOKING TOWARD THE 21ST CENTURY

George Riches

In the weeks that followed Dick Hammel's death, staff members, though grieving, often chuckled over some well-known "Hammelisms," such as: "The serious purpose of this meeting is to discuss your spelling of Hammel with one M!" Despite the jokes, the loss was deeply felt. "We lost some of the glue on the team without the Hammel style," said Chairman of the Board Curt Green, referring to his partner's talent for constructive guidance and counsel. "We had to make the adjustment to new relationships with each other to replace the glue." Accordingly, HGA's Board of Directors, president George Riches, and division directors began a series of meetings reinforcing the firm's teamwork philosophy and plotting its future course. Over the last decade, they had considerably broadened the base of the practice and with many specialists on staff were now even more determined to expand it.

The ownership changeover process that had been evolving since 1978 went into high gear immediately after Hammel's death. In accordance with the company's by-laws, the co-founder's stock was bought by the firm, thereby directly benefiting younger partners whose percentage of ownership became greater. The organization became even more democratic with new shareholders having a stronger voice.

The CADD department leaders: John Knowland, Duane Blanchard, John Pilegaard and Mike Ossian

CADD

At this point in the transition, the office instigated other changes such as advancing the computerization of the design process by investing in more computer-aided design and drafting (CADD) equipment. Management agreed that automation was a vital tool for the growing practice.

According to the three who literally ran office operations for more than 20 years — Lee Dahlen, Mary Tighe, and Vi Rice Johnson (ably assisted by Linda Anderson and Darlene Schmidt) — the old way of designing and preparing documents sometimes took as long as a year or two, depending on the job. The same work could be done in a matter of months, with the computer and other innovative time-savers.

Automated systems first came into use at HGA about 1966 — for handling correspondence,

"In health care design, we often talk about high tech vs. high touch. Today's technology means there is more and more life-saving equipment that we have to design space for. But we try to provide for the human touch, the personal side of health care with a soft warm atmosphere, a hotel-like environment."
Peter Rauma

CHAPTER X

finances, and administrative record-keeping — and were constantly updated. The first mainframe computer was installed in 1982, followed by a VAX system for the finance department, an Ethernet Local Area Network system for engineering, and in 1986, the first installation of CADD.

Architect Mike Ossian took over operations of the CADD department in 1986 and, with John Knowland and John Pilegaard trained many of HGA's architects and engineers in the effective use of the highly technical equipment. CADD gave the firm many advantages including the means of evaluating varying solutions to both architectural and engineering problems. "Architects are having to become expert and creative in their use of computer technology to stay competitive in the marketplace," said Ossian. The future is apt to bring even more revolutionary technology into architecture.

HGA Engineers Look At The Future

How do HGA engineers look at the future? They voice concerns about many issues — pollution, domestic and industrial waste, groundwater contamination, urban decay, energy conservation, and more. As director of engineering Harry Wilcox put it, "Environment is the 1990s issue — whether it's contamination of groundwater or indoor air quality." Chief civil engineer Jim Goulet added that "domestic waste and sometimes industrial wastes in landfills and dump areas are now coming back to haunt us." Engineers will play a large part in resolving these problems.

At the same time, they will have new technological advancements to help them improve the built environment. Better building materials, many man-made, will allow buildings to live longer with less maintenance; new and evolving synthetic materials will help control buried waste; geotextiles and geogrids will

Young engineers: Mark Johnson, Doug Fell, Glenn Johnson, John Bauch, Steve Makredes and Rick Hombsch

CHAPTER X

permit building placement on marginal soils; construction products will be more compatible with the environment; and new refrigerants for air conditioning will help preserve the ozone layer. According to the firm's engineering leaders, products and systems resulting from new technology will give engineers the tools they need to improve society in the years to come.

A New Generation

Throughout America, a new generation of architects, one no longer dominated by the Modernists or even the Post-Modernists, is on the scene. A variety of labels — constructivism and deconstructivism, historical preservation and hysterical conservation, high-tech and low-tech — pervades the profession. "Architecture is in a muddle," writes Brendan Gill, *The New Yorker* architecture critic. Bruce Abrahamson prefers to call it "pluralism and it is healthy," he contends. "We are not a Post-Modern firm, not totally modern, not high-tech, not minimalist, not abstract impressionist, certainly not deconstructivist or any one of the many 'isms' popular with the architectural press today. We are influenced by, in fact we experiment with, a lot of them, but we generally find our building expression and therefore, images growing out of a building's express purpose, location, and time."

Representing the new thrust in architecture is a younger HGA generation, making its own waves in the approximately 225-person firm. Some have been with the firm for more than a decade and a half, others a much shorter time. Whatever their tenure, an evolving office structure makes it possible for them to advance. In a philosophic memo, HGA president Riches wrote: "Some of us have been with HGA a long time, while many of us are new to the office. It is this blending of traditional standards, values, and

Young architects: Vince James, Loren Ahles, Joan Soranno, Tom Johnson, Dennis Wallace and Ted Rozeboom.

CHAPTER X

experiences with fresh new ideas and energy that will carry us into future growth years."

In 1989, the HGA team is a good deal larger than the founders ever dreamed. According to chief financial officer Tom Swearingen, the number of commissions and income has about tripled in the last nine years. With size has come the inevitable loss of some of the family feeling, and with expanded ownership, increasingly divergent approaches to practice have emerged. Healthy discussions about the future of the company — stressing the importance of a shared vision and the passion for building — have involved younger and older associates alike. "Although we're a group of more than 200," said vice president Michael Niemeyer, "we have a glue, a commitment that holds us together." And Curt Green asserted, "Our practice has not changed. HGA still pursues its goal of being one of the best firms in the country."

The Great Lakes Office

In keeping with the firm's strategic plan, HGA opened a branch office in Milwaukee in the fall of 1987, with associate vice presidents Steve Fiskum and Bill Kissinger in charge. "Setting up a branch there was a big step for HGA," said George Riches. "But we sensed an opportunity in the marketplace. Because we're a large firm now, we have a responsibility to our staff to provide increasing potential for growth."

By 1989, HGA's Great Lakes office staff, which included designer Jim Shields, had grown according to plan, offering full architectural services, with engineering resources primarily from the Minneapolis office. According to managing principal Fiskum, the Milwaukee office focuses on four areas — health care, corporate, educational, and local projects in a variety of locations.

Already the HGA branch is doing major medical work, office buildings, and local projects such as the Italian Community Center. Kissinger, a Milwaukee native, has high aspirations: "We hope to become the design firm of choice in this area." Despite heavy competition, managers of the new office feel the market offers great potential. "I think we must establish ourselves regionally before we become a really national firm, and that's what we're trying to do here," said Fiskum.

HGA Team Spirit

Regardless of tenure within the firm, the newest designers and engineers prefer to work in the customary HGA way — in teams. They agree with long-time staffer Bill Kokotovich, who said, "Working in a team, you draw from the excellence of everybody. Each person is responsible for sharing. It's a demo-

HGA's Great Lakes offices opened in the historic Germania Building, a Neo-Romanesque structure at 135 West Wells in Milwaukee.

"We're small now, like the way HGA began. We all wear a lot of different hats."
Steve Fiskum

"Architecture has become like designer clothing, it needs a signature."
HGA Anonymous

CHAPTER X

cratic, dynamic type of structure and, I believe, very positive. We have so much young talent in our firm, it's frightening!"

What HGA stands for is vitally important to the emerging leaders of the firm. Partner Dan Avchen, once a student of Abrahamson's and now a vice president, stressed the firm's teamwork philosophy. "We are committed to making buildings that enhance the physical environment and improve the way we live, work and play. And we do that through ideas. We pursue work together, and that's a delight because there's a lot more satisfaction about saying you are part of a successful team than saying I did it myself. That's just not the way good architecture happens. It happens at HGA through a synergy, not through an egocentric."

Over the three and one-half decades since HGA built its practice on deep-seated goals and aspirations, the original partners have witnessed a significant change in the practice of architecture. Like most American business, the profession is more competitive, more driven by the marketplace. In this complex society then, is architecture still the noble art that Hammel, Green, and Abrahamson believed in when they began? Is its purpose still as Saarinen described, "to enhance man's life on earth and help fulfill his belief in the nobility of his existence?"

Loren Ahles, vice president and director of HGA's division, believes it is. "To be an architect, you have to love to build, to improve society...by designing quality buildings. That overriding concern about quality allowed HGA in the past to go beyond the status quo. We still have these ideals and are committed to carrying them out."

Hammel Green and Abrahamson, Inc., an architectural partnership that began over a handshake 35 years ago, now pursues a national practice for the new century.

1989 Board of Directors: C. Michael Niemeyer, Kurt Rogness, Harry Wilcox, Bruce Abrahamson, Daniel Avchen, Curt Green and George Riches.

ACKNOWLEDGEMENTS

Editor
Ellen Green, E.B. Green Editorial

Production Manager
Janet Whitmore

Graphic Design
Michael J. Nelson, James E. Johnson,
James E. Johnson & Associates, Inc.

Photography
David Arkin

Lea Babcock

Richard Embery

David Guindon

George Heinrich

Thomas Hlavaty

Barbara Karant

Erich Koyama

Shin Koyama

Phillip Macmillan James

Warren Reynolds

The Architects Collaborative

Printer
Bolger Publications/Creative Printing

Typesetting
Alphagraphics One